SAVING SHELTER DOGS

TRUE SHELTER DOG STORIES, FOSTERING, VOLUNTEERING, & EVERYTHING YOU WANT TO KNOW TO RESCUE DOGS

By Mercy Lopez

EVERYTHING DOGS EDUCATION BOOK COLLECTION

Saving Shelter Dogs
True Shelter Dogs Stories, Fostering, Volunteering and Everything You Want to Know to Rescue Dogs

Everything Dogs Book Collection

By Mercy Lopez

Book design and published by
photo-video journalist, author, educator, animal advocate, activist, SAG actress/stunt woman, model, and ASCAP songwriter

Mercy Lopez

www.everythingdogs.net

ISBN   978-0-9980415-1-3

About the Author

Mercy is a first-generation Cuban/Spanish American, photojournalist, animal advocate, media influencer, foster mom, volunteer, dog rehabilitator, book author, educator and is vegan. What is really interesting about her animal adoption photography and video productions, aside from the fact that she really captures the real personality of the dogs, is that

she uses some of her original music in them.

Mercy's background in music, as a guitarist/singer/songwriter, developed in her becoming an ASCAP (American Society of Composers) and a recording artist with BMG in Berlin, Germany for 3 years.

"Show me" Video!

Binky & Sabien, "No Idea" Sunrise Music Video!

The Mercy Lopez Band Live Video!

Mercy is pictured here on the right, as a blonde, on set filming a Toyota Prius' commercial from the 90s, in South Beach!

4

She is originally from Miami, then South Beach, where she won a Harley Davidson in a beauty contest sponsored by Cristal Aguardiente and Venus Swimwear 1992. This led Mercy into modeling on the pages of Playboy, (as a blonde and a brunette), numerous videos, commercial work, BMG Germany recording artist, acting in soap operas in the Mexico DF with TV Azteca, as well as SAG acting jobs with: Oliver Stone's in *"On Any Givin Sunday"*; The Farrelly Brothers' in *"Something About Mary"*; Adam Sandler's in *"Water Boy"*; and Micheal Bays' in *"Bad Boy II" (as a* SAG/ stunt action woman). Working in these industries gave Mercy a good understanding of working with lighting and composition for her own photography and video productions.

Mercy then sold her investment property, in Little Havana, Florida to relocated to West Palm Beach, Florida, where she practiced as a commodities broker and a Realtor. She jogged and walked her dogs twice everyday, found lots of dogs, and develop a reputation as "The Dog Lady" in the neighborhood. By her coming across so many stray dogs, it led her to help dogs out many ways like volunteering and fostering at the local shelters and rescues. At one point (for a few years), she went every Sunday to her community shelter till closing. She even got locked in the kennel adoption floor a lot, because it was hard for her to leave. Helping dogs keeps Mercedes/Mercy very busy and it is especially rewarding to her when, she see's the faces of rescued pets together with their new forever family.

With the great support she received from social media and happy adoptions, it encouraged Mercy to spend about 5 years of her extra time, into getting her new book collection just right to publish. It has more detail than, she has in her previously published 15 mini iBooks. It's everything she thinks that's important for every dog guardian or animal lover.

She admits that volunteering can be challenging work that, has left her with some very unsettling experiences. This is why writing these books brought Mercy lots of healing by honoring so many dogs she worked with and their memories here. It is apparent

that, every dog she has worked with has deeply touched her heart.

Mercy says, "It's very important to attract attention by generating media interest in animal issues like sterilization programs, dog training, assisting animals in our communities, finding successful homes and most importantly, to reduce animal intake and euthanasia in shelters everywhere". With photography, video and social media, she knows that we can reach the masses, for successful adoptions and sterilization. She sees positive improvements every year!

It is very apparent on Mercy's Facebook page, that her passion burns deep with enthusiasm and she is full of positive optimism.

She hopes that her work encourages you to help out animals in some way.

Just click on the blue links to check out some of her videos and get to know her awesome furry friends!

Avery's Adoption Video and Hannah's Adoption Video!.

CBS "Pet of the Day" with Avery & Hannah

Facebook Live, CBS 12 "Pet of the Day" Video!

Mercy's Portfolio Pictures
On the previous page from left to right, going down:

- With Oliver Stone, on set filming "On Any Given Sunday"
- With Henry Winkler and Adam Sandler on set filming "Water Boy"
- Mercedes as Black Widow series model for Marble, Wizard and Max Comic Books, by Greg Horn
- With LL Cool Jay on "Any Given Sunday"
- With Lenny Kravitz
- Germany BMG "Show Me" music video
- Mercy Lopez Band performing in Berlin
- Black Widow Cover
- Toyota Prius Commercial with a pink dog
- "Universal Soldier" with Jean-Claude Van Dam
- Guitarist for Luis Enrique, Universal music
- Playboy September 1992's, "Girls of South Beach".With Mr. Olympia Bob Paris. Catalog work in Cancun, Mexico
- Pepsi

Mercy's Foster, Stella's Story
<u>Stella's Story Video</u>

<u>Mercy's Singing Dogs Here!</u>

Introduction
Everything Dogs Book Collection

Everything Dogs Series Introduction Video

Everything Dogs 15 Minutes Mini Movie Here!

Everything Dogs Collection Book Project is based on true shelter dog photography and video stories (with original music from the author-publisher), combined with detailed research of everything pet guardians and animal lovers should know about dogs.

Everything Dog's was designed to: enhance our relationship with dogs, reduce animal intake, assist eliminate euthanasia numbers in shelters, educate on today's animal overpopulation situation in shelters in the United State's, encourage: fostering, volunteering, sterilization, adopting, basic dog training and humane holistic health maintenance animal care, even during a pet emergency.

All of the collections books contain many pet guardians tips that, can lead to an enhanced, positive, safe and loving relationship with your furry family member.

Proceeds of Everything Dogs Book Collection education books go to animal rescue charity partners.

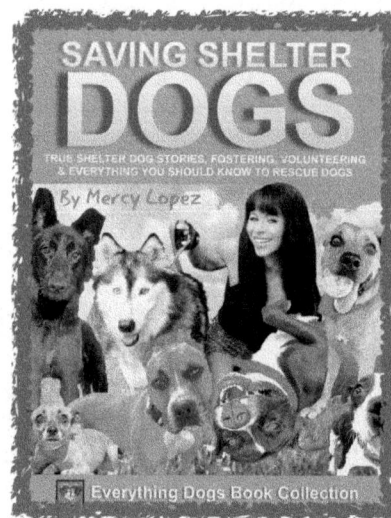

Here are some of the popular topics that this book *"Saving Shelter Dogs - True Shelter Dog Stories, Fostering, Volunteering & Everything You Should Know to Rescue Dogs"* goes over in detail:

The Truth About Animal Shelters, True Shelter Dog Stories (with videos and full-color pictures stories), Statistics, Fostering, Volunteering, Anti-Tethering Law, Condition of Intake Dogs, Common Choking Collar Accidents, Lost/Stray and Found Animals, What We are Doing to Bring our Animal Intake and Euthanasia Numbers Down, Sterilization, Euthanasia, High-Risk Animals, Black Dog Syndrome, Kennel-Mates Save Lives, Foster Dog Stories, Playgroup-Playing for Life Program, Count Down to Zero Initiative Program, Pitbull History, Breed Specific Legislation (BSL), How we are Saving Lives in our Communities and more!

Other Everything Dogs Book Collections includes:

- **Getting Started on the Right Paw - Basic Dog Training - Introducing Your New Dog to Your Home, Other Pets and more!** Includes:

How to Pick the Right Pet Together as a Family, Statistics, What to Consider When Adopting a Dog, True Shelter Dog's Pictures and Video Stories Links, Children and Dogs, How to Introduce Your New Dog to Your Home and Other Exciting Pets, How to Doggie Proof Your Home and Yard, How To Get Ready for Your New Dog to Come Home, Safety, House Training, Chewing, Leaving Pets Home Alone, How to Avoid Bathroom Accidents, Basic Dog Training, Placement, Rewards for Your Dogs, Basic Commands, Leash Pulling, Heel and more!

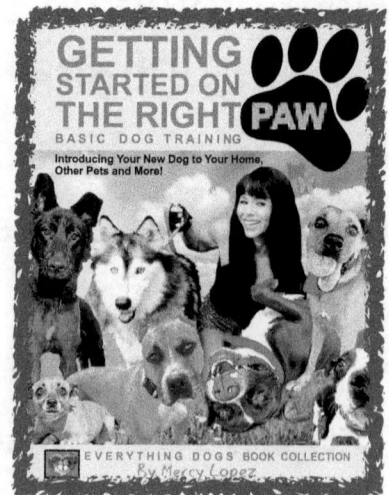

•**Dogs Holistic Health Maintenance and Remedies Encyclopedia:**

This book goes over the details of: Dog Holistic Healing, Natural Alternatives, Essential Oils, Herbs, Natural Repellents, Different Skin Conditions, Hot Spots, Yeast, Staff Infection, Demodex, Natural Holistic Fleas and Ticks, Prevention and Natural

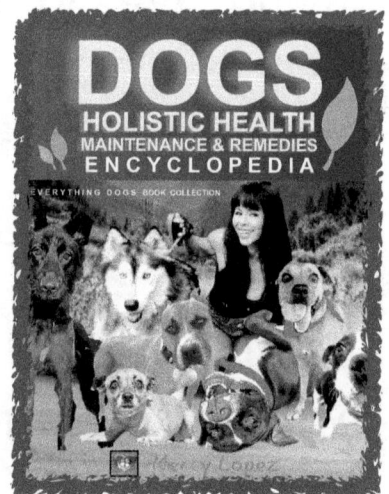

Alternatives, Ears, Eyes, Teeth, Gums, Older Dog's Health, Super Healing Roots, Super-Greens Supplementation, Benefits of Basic Herbs, Herbal Tonic Remedies, Vaccines, Holistic Alternatives and Remedies, Heartworms, Natural Prevention for Flea, Tick, Heartworm and Mosquitos for your Lawn and Home, Homeopathic Do It Yourself Sprays, Vaccines, Medications, Foods You Can and Can Not Feed Your Dogs, Gluten-Free Grains, Prebiotic, Probiotics, Live Enzymes, Leaky Gut, Basic Nutrition Your Dog Needs on a Vegan Diet, Dog Health Maintenance and Holistic Natural Alternative Remedies, pH Balance, What is in Your Pet's Food, Nutrition, Vegan Food Full Color Pictures, and Recipes.

•**Dog Emergencies** - What to do in a Common Pet Emergency:

Dog's Emergencies is a quick training manual to prepare you in case of a rescue emergency with your pet or any dog that may need your fast action assistance.

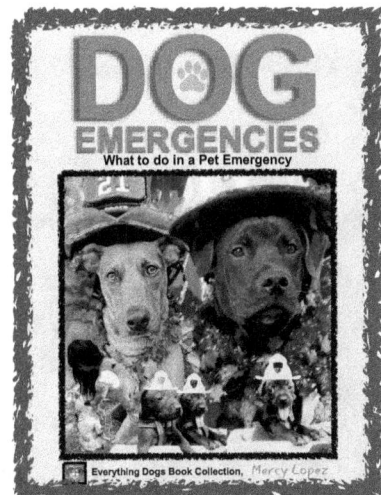

It goes over: Most Common Pet Emergencies, How to Respond,

Rescue Protocols, First Aid, What to do if your dog is Over-Heating, How to Perform Heimlich maneuver if your dog is choking, CPR/Cardiopulmonary Resuscitation on your pet, Safety demonstration videos more!

I hope that you will look at animal overpopulation in your own back yard, differently, and compassionately.

After volunteering at shelters, I am more aware of the truth that, takes place in animal shelters. I just wanted to share with you a little bit of what the dogs are like, based on my experience, their story and dedicate this to all the souls of animals that never walk out of a shelter alive. After collecting tremendous amounts of dog pictures, Everything Dogs books honor their memory in hopes that, it

moves someone like you, to save a dog or help. No animal's life should end shortly because, they don't have a home or space in the shelter.

Warning: This inspiring education book may cause a sudden urge to start saving dog's lives. You might even end up being a possible foster failure!

Open your heart to fostering, volunteering, donating and adopting. All animals can enhance your life, bring your happiness and even benefit your health!

Special Dedication to Binky

On June 1, 2011, I was walking my dogs before heading to a yoga class. My neighbor approached me with this beautiful black and white, female, Pitbull mix dog. He had just found her in the vacant lot next to us. He gave her to me because, he knew I was a dog person and saw me walking my two dogs every day, twice a day. I named her "Binky". She was about a year old, so cute, sweet and beautiful that, I could not resist, to immediately help her out. I brought her home, gave her food, water and took

care of her, until I could hopefully get her back to her owners. I got her immediately scanned for a microchip, but she did not have one, or any identification tag. I followed the legal protocol for lost and found dogs. I thought someone must be missing and/or looking for her because of the red collar she had on, so followed found dog protocol. I quickly starting to put up lost/found dog flyers and signs everywhere, so she would be visible for her family to find her. I took advantage of all the free ads in the major local newspapers. I also posted her picture on the Palm Beach County Animal Care and Control website page; under found dog like you are supposed to do, so that lost dogs can be reunited.

For days, we covered the entire area for miles to find her family, but no one had seen her before or knew who she belonged to, During this time, she became part of my pack of dogs and we fell in love with her. *This was Binky's First Picture that I posted to find her guardians.*

After 10 days, I received a call from Animal Care and Control telling me to bring Binky in that, I can adopt her by putting a "reserve adoption hold" so I could take her back home with me.

When I brought her to Animal Care and Control, they asked me to wait for her while they checked her out privately. When they came back out, I was handed Binky's new collar and leash. I was told that Binky had to be put on a 10-day hold at the shelter to allow her legal guardian the opportunity to find her and start the 10 day process again. I was heartbroken. I was even more confused when, they told me that, I could not see or visit her while she was there. I thought How is her family going to find her? This was a very difficult realization. While I was there I observed how our community "kill shelters" are understaffed and under-budgeted. This, in turn, lacks to provide animals the attention, space, care they need and deserve.

City commissioners set out budgets for county departments and the last departments they consider funding are the ones that don't have a voice; like the animal service divisions known as animal control shelters in our community.

Finally, Binky's 10 days of being locked up in an unfamiliar scary kennel were over. I returned to Palm Beach County Animal Care and Control to rush my adoption application through; to get my "Stinky Binky" out. They told me again that, I could not see her and I would have to wait for an inspector to come out to my property (this took another 2 weeks). Finally, the inspection was complete. At this point, she was ready for surgery to get spayed/sterilized for final adoption with me. After her surgery, I still could not see or take her home. Apparently, she was bleeding internally, due to a towel she ate that, she

was still passing. I believe she eat the towel out of boredom, mind deteriorating and by not getting the attention she mentally and physically needed in a confined kennel space for such a long time. During this time, she developed Canine Infectious Respiratory Disease (CIRD), also known as Kennel Cough or a doggie cold. It's very similar to a human cold and very common. If she had the Bordatella vaccination given by her previous owner veterinarian, it would have prevented her from getting sick. Her time was running out at the shelter, when, I finally got a call saying that, "if you want her, then come get her now!".

Of course, I rushed to pick her up! On June 21, 2011, she officially became a member of our family. This was the longest month of my life. Aside from what she went through, her dramatic experience of being separated from me like that, but also she was

taking up unnecessary space in a kill shelter that, could have kept some dogs alive.

Everything Dogs Series Introduction Video

Check out a video clip of when Binky was given back to me and the special magical connection we had. How she recognized me and how we felt about one another. She was so excited and happy.

Through volunteering at a shelter, I later became friends with that same staff member who gave Binky back to me. She said she remembered that moment because, she had never seen a dog be so happy being pick up like that before; showing so much love to a stranger. Not knowing that, I had her with me for a short while and brought her in.

Soon after this experience, I decided to look into how I could help animals in my community at this particular kill shelter, even though I had volunteered

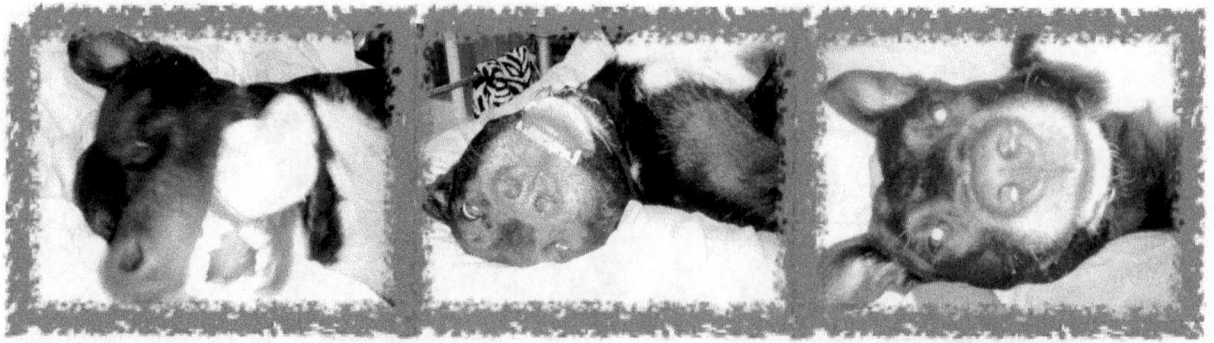

at other local animal rescue organizations. The more I saw, the more I realized that I had to somehow do more! Binky opened my eyes to how animals suffer in shelters because, of the current system in place and lack of sterilization. People say it is difficult to help out, so they just don't help out at all. We can change this attitude by showing in these books that, there are many different ways to help animals in dire need in your area. By giving a little bit of your time, love and affection to a shelter, or rescue organizations we can turn this awful animal overpopulation situation into a more positive one.

Binky was four years old when in the middle of the night she mysteriously started coughing up blood. The morning before she went for a jog alongside me as, I rollerbladed up the street, of course, I immediately rushed to get her the best help that, I could. I was scheduled to filming CBS - Channel 12's "Pet of the Day" that next morning. I was faced with having to drop my Binky off at the veterinarian to run some tests and be separated from her for the first time since, our animal control experience. She had veterinarian check-up's a month before, showing that she was healthy. They gave a Heartworm preventative treatment injection for her first time. With this being said, I could not imagine anything being wrong with her but wondered if the heartworm prevention shot had something to do with this.

I took Binky to 4 different veterinarian specialist and we gave her every test that could help her available. No test or doctor could explain to us why her lungs were filling up so fast! They took out a minimum of 850 cc's of bloody fluid from her lungs each time (above pictures). She needed five emergency surgeries to drain the blood out of her lungs. She also had two blood transfusions from "Apollo" (on right) from GTS Husky Rescue.

Apollo and I on "CBS Pet of the Day" Video!

During the course of the next ten days of her suffering, Binky could

no longer lay down. It was as if she was drowning and suffocating from the blood filling up in her lungs. We could not sleep at all from holding her up so that, she could get some relief and rest while sleeping sitting up. Her lungs continued to refill faster every day with more blood, every breath for her was a struggle. You could hear the liquid build-up gurgling in her lungs. It was devastating for our family. Dr. Martin from Jupiter Animal Health Clinic worked with her endlessly, hoping that we could find out what was wrong with her to save her.

Some of the tests available would take two weeks for the results to get back to us. Time Binky didn't have. We treated her with vitamin K, thinking maybe she ate some poison and with "Yunnan Baiyao" (a hard to find Chinese herb, used during the Vietnam war to help stop bleeding). It changed the color of

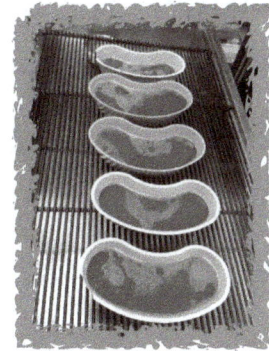

the fluid in her lungs, as you can see in the pictures shown above.

We did our best to figure out the mystery of why her lungs were disintegrating like gel. It was killing her! During this time, I learned that the veterinary field had its limitation. This may have been beneficial for my Binky at the time.

On November 21, 2014, Binky went into her last emergency surgery. Her last specialist veterinarian had installed tubes with knobs on each side of her, into her lungs in desperate measures to save her. This was so that, I could drain out the excess fluids in her lungs and help her breath. Her lungs kept on filling up with more bloody fluid, faster each day. We knew it was a very dangerous and sensitive procedure, but we thought this could help buy more time while we find out what was wrong and how to treat her. She needed medical intervention. We were running out of options for fighting off blood infections and transfusion risks. Her doctor said that she tried to take 2 breaths and died coming out of the anesthesia from surgery. I had a few moments with her and saw all the knobs and tubes sticking out of her in the attempt to save her. I never saw a dog fight so hard to live! I have never done so much in an attempt to keep a dog alive in such a short period of time.

After the necropsy, which is an autopsy for dogs, the doctor's opinion of the cause of death was idiopathic, meaning "unexplainable". They found that the blood clots and infection from the blood in her lungs was conclusive with what were going on with her. I still have no explanation as to what happened to my Binky. We could not find out why her lungs reacted this way. Maybe if there was more research, Binky would have lived a long life. I wish that we could have at least know what happened that, caused her lungs to disintegrate into a gel.

The mystery of what happened to my Binky still haunts me and remains in my memory. This experience still haunts me!

Because of what I have learned about the overall mentality of our government that mandates excessive vaccines, the animal maintenance care industry (controlled by animal pharmaceuticals, plus large pet foods corporations preservatives in packaged foods) is possibly poisoning our pets. I believe that there are links to why so many dogs are commonly getting cancer at alarming numbers.

I know that there is a great deal of room for research and improvements for the advancement of veterinary medicine. I had another dog; "Ralph", that also had issues with lung cancer; as well as my "Joy Bird", that died of cancer. One of my dogs, "Hawkeye", died from eating a commercially sold rawhide. Manufactures knows rawhide commonly kills dogs and they continue to sell them! I'm thinking, "Could some of this be relevant to the pet foods that we feed our pets? Maybe there is a link with vaccines? Do you wonder too?

I now look at everything pertaining to dogs' health differently since, my experience with Binky. I question the dog health industries, the consumer products that are made available and advertised in today's modern convenient package food industry.

So, I did extensive research for my own dogs' health and maintenance so that I can bring to you the **"*Dogs Holistic Health Maintenance and Remedies Encyclopedia*"** book. I highly recommend for: health wellness conscious animal lover friends.

Binky's passing away inspired me in many ways. Aside from helping at dog shelters and I also took a "foster challenge". I fostered five dogs in honor of the five surgical attempts to try to save Binky. As of now, I have surpassed that goal and have found many pets awesome safe homes. I now hope to raise money and to promote animal awareness with Everything Dogs Book Collection Project to help families and pooches!

My last picture with my "Binky" (bottom right) after her 4th surgery attempt trying to save her.

Binky Rounding Up Chickens!

Sabien & Binky Singing Together!

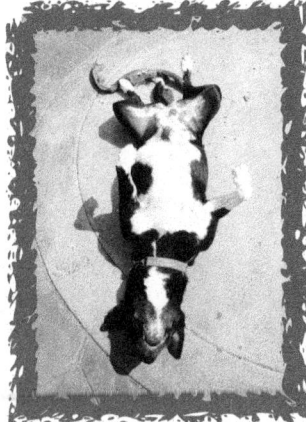

Ralph & Rodger

Love you & always in my heart. RIP.

I've had other dogs than Binky that had suffered from lung cancer and wonder why it is so common for dogs if they don't smoke. Could it be linked to the food that is sold to us commercially that is loaded with toxic preservatives, the additives, synthetic ingredient for the manufacture to meet the standard of nutrition to be sold to us because they are cooked at such high temperature that it kills the nutrition and that cause harm?

Special Thanks

I want to thank my: Binky, Sabien, Hawkeye, Joy Bird, Mac, Ralph, Blankie, Benji, Broggie, Harley and Davidson. As well as my foster failures: Juno, Pretzel, Rodger, Mindy, and Coco for continuing to inspire me. They filled my heart with love.

I wish everyone could experience as many awesome memories with their furry family members too!

Thank you for taking the time to invest in your dogs and for your interest in the world of Everything Dogs Education Collection Books!

Kim Tunney Johnson

I want to give recognition to this very talented, speedy, co-proofing editor. She is very sharp in the field of being a paralegal and is always multi-tasking. She has full custody of her adopted, sweet, beautiful granddaughter "Karina". She used to have more time to foster urgent status dogs and help out at the shelter. She helped save "Hope", a blind dog's life, that is now happily re-homed. Kim was a victim of her own dog being stolen by a burglar from home. She has never fully recovered from the loss of her furry loved one. She is an animal activist and is always helping out dogs; in the best ways that she can.

Disclaimer

Everything Dogs Book Collection is based on true rescue dog stories. It is intended for public education, to help families develop a lasting and healthy relationship with their pets. I feel if people can implement some of the information in these books, we can compassionately bring our animal intake and euthanasia numbers down in high kill shelters.

The publisher and author are not responsible for any specific health, or any allergy needs that may require medical supervision and not liable for any damages, or negative consequences from any treatments, actions, applications or preparations to any pet or person in regards to the reading or following any of the information contained in this book.

For diagnosis or treatment of any medical situation, always consult your professional veterinarian immediately.

Neither the publisher nor the individual author shall be liable for any physical, psychological, emotional, financial or commercial damages. Including, but not

Table of Content

Chapter 3 125
How we are Bringing our Euthanasia Numbers Down 125

Chapter 1
The Truth About
Animal Shelters

Warning: this action dog video might make you want to take volunteering, fostering, donating or an adoption challenge!

These video experiences are a positive view on what an amazing difference you can have to these shelter dogs, as well as its super rewarding benefit to your heart and soul!

Everything Dog Introduction VIdeo

Everything Dogs 15 Minutes Mini Movie Here!

A True Life of a Shelter Dog Video!

Shelter Dogs Having a Good Time Video!

Ali's Adoption Video!

Shelter Statistics

This picture above was taken at my local shelter Palm Beach County Animal Care and Control front desk lobby / customer service on June 30,2013.

It shows year to date that their were 8,364 animal intake and 4,677 of euthanized animals here alone. They no longer have this display.

(WTXL) - Florida had one of the highest numbers of cats and dogs killed at shelters in 2019, according to this latest study.

The study was conducted by Best Friends Animal Society found that in 2018, 352,000 cats and dogs entered shelters in the state of Florida, 262,000 were saved and 55,400 were killed.

It also only found 40 no-kill communities in Florida.

According to the study, Florida was behind California, Texas, and North Carolina.

This study done in 2019 showed: over 55,400 dogs and cats were killed in Florida shelters last year, simply because they didn't have safe places to call home.

The study found over 2,000 dogs and cats in America are killed every day in shelters.

Together, we can change this and achieve no-kill for dogs and cats nationwide by 2025.

2017-2018

76.% of cats and dogs were saved, up 2.8% of 2017 data.

5,325,077 entered in shelters

4,093,735 were saved

732,732,797 were killed

88% shelter data know

- There are about 13,600 community animal shelters nationwide that are all independent. There is no national organization monitoring these shelters.

- 88% of U.S. households, or about 85 million families, own a pet; according to the 2017-2018 National Pet Owners Survey conducted by the American Pet Products Association (APPA). This is up from 56% of U.S. households in 1988. This was the first year the survey was conducted.

- Approximately 7.6 million companion animals enter animal shelters nationwide every year (down from 13 million in 1973). Of those, approximately **3.9 million** are dogs and 3.4 million are cats.

- Each year, approximately 2.7 million animals are euthanized; **1.2 million dogs** and 1.4 million cats.

- Tragically, 4 million of these homeless pets are killed each year in America's shelter.

- More than 7 animals per minute are killed in shelters unnecessarily across the country. This means more than 9,000 animals per day.

- Due to the efforts of dedicated hard-working staff and volunteers, euthanasia rates are about half of what they were in 1970, but we still have a long way to go, as shown by the numbers that don't lie.

- **50% of shelter animals were relinquished by their owners**

- 20% of the people who relinquish their dogs to the shelter, adopted them from a shelter

- 50% of shelter animals were picked up as strays

- 10% of dogs taken into shelters have been spayed or neutered.

- About 9.6 million animals are euthanized annually in the United States

- 60% of shelter dogs are euthanized

- 70% of shelter cats are euthanized

- 5,000 shelters in the United States

- 14,000 animals were euthanized in 2012, in Palm Beach County, Florida.

Florida Shelter Statistics

According to Animal Services; **Miami Dade Animal Control Services** in Florida, in the 1960s, about one

quarter of the dog population was still roaming the streets (whether owned or not) and 10 to 20-fold more dogs were euthanized in shelters compared to the present. Current data from across the United

States support the idea that, along with increased responsible pet ownership behaviors, sterilization efforts in shelters and private veterinary hospitals have played a role driving and sustaining the decline in unwanted animals entering shelters (and being euthanized). Additionally, data shows that adoption numbers are rising slowly across the US and have become an additional driver of declining euthanasia numbers in the last decade.

Recently in Miami Dade Animal Shelter more than 37,000 animals come in and out of their shelter each year. Around 6,000 get adopted, rescue missions find homes for about 8,000 of them and the rest are euthanized.

For the past 25 years, the problem has remained constant: More than 20,000 animals are euthanized each year in Miami-Dade County alone. More than 90 percent of them are perfectly healthy and ready to be adopted.

Broward County Animal 2015
Intake: 14,868
Euthanized and kennel deaths: 5,964
Save rate: 59.89%

Broward Humane Society 2015

Total Intake: 9730

Euthanized/kennel deaths: 6,233

Save rate: 36%

Includes taking in 1099 dogs from out of Florida.

Palm Beach County Animal Control 2015

Total Intake: 13,366

Euthanized or died: 5,582

Save rate: 41.76%

The number of dogs and cats killed at Palm Beach County's animal shelter has plummeted by 19 percent over the last year. Marking this the first time the facility has seen such a large dip since it first opened in the late 1960's. The euthanasia rate among cats was down by 24%, while the number of unwanted dogs killed dropped by 3%.

About 45-50 animals are taken in each day at *Palm Beach County Animal Care and Control.*

- **25% of dogs in shelters are adopted**

- **15% of dogs in shelters are reunited with their owners**

- 2% of cats in shelters are reunited with their owners

- 20% of dogs adopted from shelters are returned, 50% within the first 2 weeks

- 19% of owned dogs came from a shelter

- 22% of owned cats came from a shelter

- 54% of shelters report "Big Black Dog Syndrome", which keeps black dogs in shelters much longer and are at a higher risk.

- 70 million estimated stray cats in the U.S.

- 80 million is the number of cats that can be produced from one mated pair and their offspring in 10 years

- The majority of pets are obtained from acquaintances and family members

- **28% of dogs are purchased from breeders, and 29% of cats and dogs are adopted from shelters and rescues**

- **More than 35% of cats are acquired as strays. (Source: APPA)**

According to the *American Humane Association*, the most common reasons why people relinquish or give away their dogs is because; their place of residence does not allow pets (29%), not enough time, divorce, death and behavioral issues (10% each). The most common reasons for cats was that they were not allowed in the residence (21%) and allergies (11%).

Pet Overpopulation and Facts

It is impossible to determine how many stray dogs and cats live in the United States. The estimates for cats alone range up to 70 million.

- The average number of litters a fertile *cat* produces is one to two per year; the average number of kittens is four to six per litter.

- The average number of litters that fertile *dogs* produce is one a year; the average number of puppies is four and in many cases 10 or more.

- Owned cats and dogs generally live longer healthier lives than strays

- Many strays are lost pets who were not kept properly indoors or provided with identification

- Only 10% of the animals received by shelters have been spayed or neutered, while 83% of pet dogs and 91% of pet cats are spayed or neutered.

Top 10 Reasons
For Relinquishment Dogs

Moving (7%)

Landlord not allowing pets (6%)

Too many animals in the household (4%)

Cost of pet maintenance (5%)

Owner having personal problems (4%)

Inadequate facilities (4%)

No homes available for litter mates (3%)

Having no time for pet (4%)

Pet illness (4%)

Biting (3%)

Top 10 Reasons
For Relinquishment Cats

Moving (8%)

Landlord not allowing pets (6%)

Too many animals in the household (11%)

Cost of pet maintenance (6%)

Owner having personal problems (4%)

Inadequate facilities (2%)

No homes available for litter mates (6%)

Allergies in family (8%)

House soiling (5%)

Incompatibility with other pets (2%)

Characteristics of Relinquished Pets

- The majority of the surrendered dogs (47.7%), and cats (40.3%) were between 5 months and 3 years of age.

- The majority of dogs (37.1%) and cats (30.2) had been owned from 7 months to 1 year.

- Approximately, half of the pets (42.8% of dogs; 50.8% of cats) surrendered were not neutered. Many of the pets relinquished (33% of dogs; 46.9% of cats) had not been to a veterinarian.

- Animals acquired from friends were relinquished in higher numbers (31.4% of dogs; 33.2% of cats) than from any other source.

- Close to equal numbers of male and female dogs and cats were surrendered.

- Most dogs (96%) had not received any obedience training.

This study is conducted by the NCPPSP - National Council on Pet Population Study and Policy.

Lost and Found

This happy reunion picture, of the tan dog kissing and bringing an amazing smile to this gentleman,

was taken at Palm Beach County Animal Care and Control, when pet owner found his dog after straying away from home. The owner did not want to get his dog sterilized and was happy to pay a high fee to Animal Control to get his dog back registered un-sterilized.

Keep in mind, when you see a loose or lost dog, that they may be someone's family pet. A family may be worried sick about them. Perhaps the lost a dog may need medicine, the can get hit by a car rendered helpless, maybe someone steals and sells them, or hurt them. They may have: anxiety, fear, may not like strangers approaching them and can be dangerous if approached

Your local animal control or rescues can help find them get back to their home or find them a home.

Please use caution. If you choose to lure a stray dog with food or treats, not all dogs are friendly and can react by biting or attacking you. Always act for the well-being of the animal's safety.

Lost Dog Check List

•Contact your local animal control facility for help with a lost animal, and post a picture of the lost, or found a dog in their system or website. So that if someone is looking for them, you can be in contacted.

- Your local newspaper may be able to accommodate you on a free ad for found dogs.

- In case you have found a dog and have a person claiming their pet, have them provide proof of recent vaccination and ownership.

I strongly advise against contacting the police. They don't have the training yet to handle loose dog situations. They are known at times to handle a situation in defense, resulting in fatal shooting to the animal. The police are not the proper animal authority.

Any information that you can provide about the lost animal; including photos or videos with date and time recorded stamp if the dog has a collar, what color, special markings and sex, can be very helpful.

Dogs often stray and run off if left in a yard alone, by digging under or jumping over a fence, to explore. This commonly results in dogs getting fatally hit by cars or ending up at the shelter in bad condition.

Keeping or Adopting a Stray Dog

Section 4-8. It shall be unlawful for any person in the county to harbor or keep any stray or lost animal unless he/she has notified the Division *within twenty-four (24) hours from the time such an animal came into his/her possession*. Upon receiving such notice, the Division may require the person to bring the animal to the Division for identification or sheltering, if necessary. It shall be unlawful for any person to refuse to surrender any

such stray animal to an authorized representative of the Division upon demand of such representative.
(b) Adopting stray found animals.

The Division, at its sole discretion, may permit residents who possess a stray dog or cat and who wish to provide it a permanent home to legally adopt such animal by adhering to the following procedures:

(1) Take the stray animal to the Division to be **scanned for an electronic animal identification device (EAID) and checked for a tattoo.** *Proof must be presented* to the Division that these requirements have been met.

2) *Complete an official division **"found" form,*** which provides all appropriate identifying information for the animal. Such animal(s) may become the property of a person if the following requirements are also met: a) Photographs and identifying information have been posted at the Division for **ten (10) working days.** b) The animal has been given a **rabies inoculation and County tag.** c) The animal has been sterilized, and the animal has been implanted with an electronic animal identification device (EAID). The requirements herein must be

secured within thirty (30) calendar days after the Division approves the adoption application. Extensions may be granted by the Division for reasonable requests. Any deviation from these adoption requirements by the potential adopter will void the adoption.

At its discretion, the Division may refuse adoption of an animal, if it is determined that the adoption is not in the best interest of the animal, or the health, safety or the general welfare of the public.

Dizzy

Born blind, this smart and sweet pitbull mix, brindle mix. Dizzy was an owner surrender to the shelter. He was adopted! He looked like he was always looking at me.

Angelia Jolie's Story

She was brought to me by someone that saw her every day on their way to work. They thought she was left outside, of what appeared to be an abandoned house, without food or water. I thought it was suspicious that someone would bring me a dog and not contact the proper animal authority themselves. So, I followed the protocol and had her scanned as soon as I got her. She had no microchip, no identification and no rabies tag on her. She tested

positive for skin demodex, which I found a sponger for her treatment. There was no way to know if her vaccines or heartworm treatments were up to date. When the dog's owner discovered her dog was missing, she spoke to a neighbor that led her to the person that was working down the street and took the dog from her property. The pet owner threaten to call the police to report it, which could cause the person, who brought aka Angelina to me (this is what I called her), to lose his job and go to jail. I encourage him to contact animal control directly. They allowed me to give this dog back to him, to give her back to her owner immediately. During my time fostering her, I trained her to sit and walk on a leash. This always helps dogs have a better chance of getting adopted. She had so much energy.

Use caution when assuming responsibility over stray dogs and keep in mind the many liability issues. If you find a stray dog, always keep in mind it may belong to a good family, looking for them for a long time.   Call or better yet, go to your   local animal control facility for help with a stray animal.

This dogs mouth and nose was tied shut.

Pregnant Dog & Bad Shape Dog Found Story Video Video!

Mercedes Lopez-Roberson
OCTOBER 21

Same Location Brown Stray Dog Stray Pitbull Hit by Train

Emaciated Scared Rescue Dog Video!
January 23, 201

Anti-Tethering Law

Flower at the Shelter

The Palm Beach County Board of County Commissioners approved an amendment to the existing County Ordinance on tethering animals. As of September 1, 2003, it is unlawful to chain or

FLOWER
ID #A172190
Learning to Trust Again!

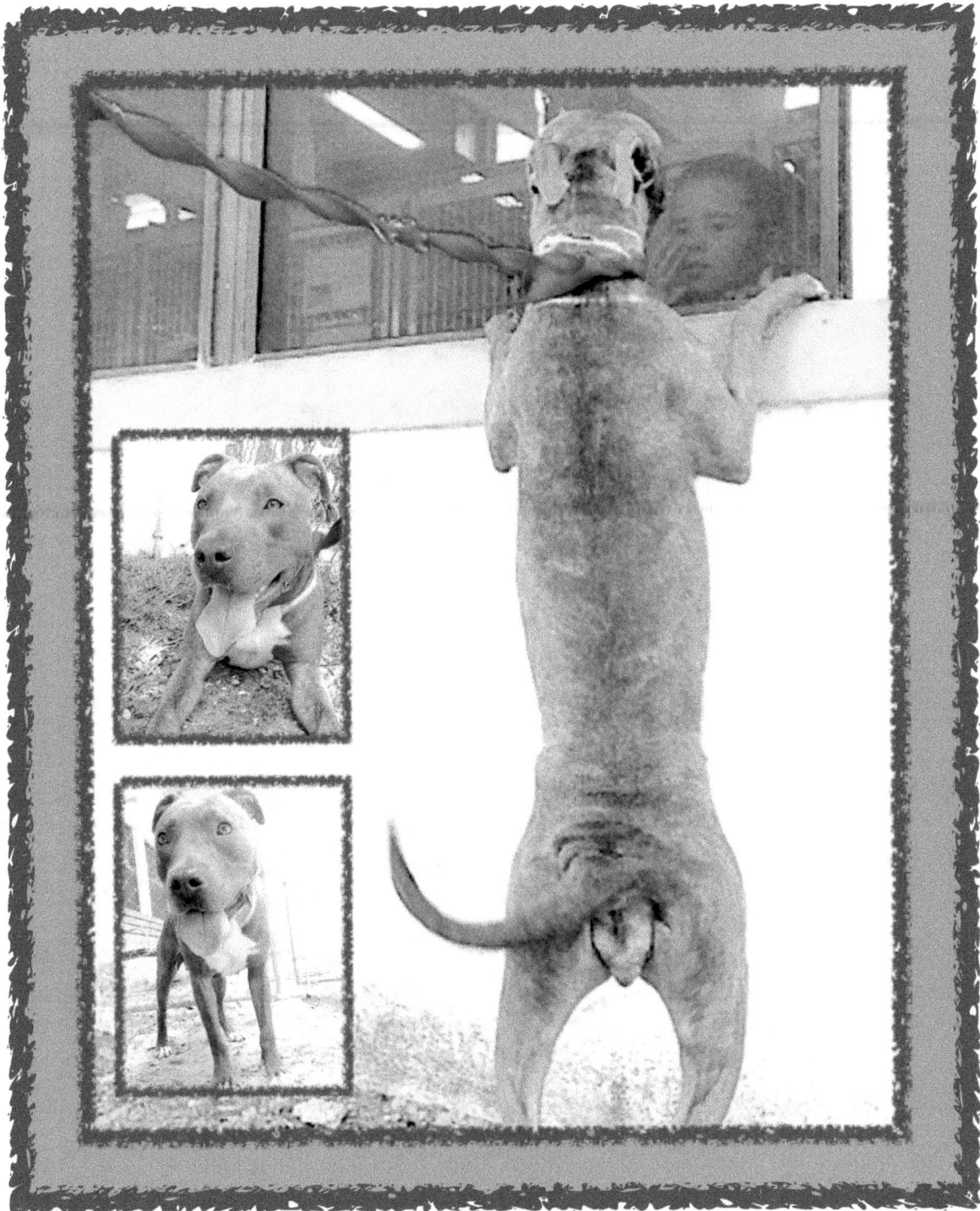

tether your dog outdoors between the hours of 10:00 AM and 5:00 PM (County Ordinance 2003-029) When Palm Beach County Animal Care and Control receives complaints about dogs tied up outdoors, officials will respond and issue a violation warning during the first visit. It is important that residents calling in a complaint to be very specific about the address and identification of the animal(s) being tied up during the specified times.

Tethered Dogs

Lengthy exposure to extremely cold or hot weather can be fatal to a dog. They could get tangled in the tether/chain. It can cause aggression towards humans and other animals, mental stress, poor socialization and lack of companionship. The dog will become territorial. Being left outside in a storm causes anxiety and fear. Health deterioration, skin problems (can occur from constant tethering) and constant exposure to the elements is dangerous.

Strangulation by Dog Collar

Dog collar accidents are very common resulting in death. Wearing dog collars can be hazardous in the wrong situation. Dog collars and tags can become entangled or caught between many things like the wires of his or her crate, kitchen cabinets, fencing or furniture. Even while playing with another dog, it can be very dangerous for both dogs and you. Dogs can jump up and snag their collar on a fence post, a window latch or blinds, leading to strangulation.

Even a well-fitting collar can be dangerous if used to tie up a dog in the backyard. It's common for dogs who are tied up to jump fences while tied on a long leash and end up hanging themselves with their collar.

When a dog panics, this can cause a dog to choke himself. You will likely need very sharp scissors or a knife to cut the collar off.

Strangulation by collar is very common and has caused many dogs to lose their lives.

Dog Collars Accidents are Common

Large pet retail companies created break-away collars because of dogs choking with their collar are so common. **Break-Away Collars** are highly recommended. Make sure it is reliable because some brands can easily snap and become open. If this happens, you may have a loose dog situation.

Strict dog collar removal policies are set in place, in many pet-related businesses, to remove collars from dogs, such as:

• For a veterinary technician, it is mandatory to remove all collars, from all patients in a kennel.

• Large retail grooming chains have strict policies requiring dog collars to be removed before dogs are placed in their kennels. Their collars are then placed in a plastic sleeve outside of the dog's crate.

Dogs should only wear a collar under supervision. This means you should take your dog's collar off whenever they're crated, playing with other dogs, or left unsupervised in your home.

Too Loose or Tight Collars

Loose Collars - Known to cause limb or mouth injuries. When a pet scratches their ear, back leg or front leg could get stuck inside the collar, or looped through, leading to a limb breaking. Dogs can also get their teeth or tongue stuck in a collar as well while grooming themselves. This could lead to broken teeth and other mouth injuries.

Tight Collar - A collar that is too tight can be harmful to a dog. This could also lead to skin irritation and hair loss. The skin in those areas can be more prone to infection.

- In extreme cases, a very tight collar can cut into a dog's neck. This can happen in cases of neglect, when a puppy collar is left on a growing dog, or abandoned for long periods and neglected.

- In general, to protect your pup's neck, regularly check that the collar still fits well. It's recommended to let your dog sleep at night without a collar so that your dog's skin can air out.

- A chest harness or "Gentle Leader" can be a safer alternative to neck collars that put a lot of strain on a dog's neck.

Neck Damage

Collars can harm a dog's neck if you pull too hard on the leash, or if you use the collar to pull your dog around. The neck and throat are extremely sensitive areas. Repeated stress on the neck can even lead to long-term medical issues, including damaging the thyroid glands, tissues around the neck area and salivary glands.

General Discomfort

Even if a collar does not lead to any serious injuries, the wrong collar can simply be irritating for a dog. Pet owners should avoid a collar that looks rigid and uncomfortable because your dog should have a positive experience when are wearing them and enjoy the feeling.

Collar Safety Tips

When sizing a collar, make sure you can fit your thumb between the collar and the dog's neck. If the dog sits down or rolls over, their skin and body fat is redistributed, possibly resulting in the collar being too tight.

Constricting Collars

Keep it loose enough, so you can slip two fingers under the collar. If your dog pulls excessively on the leash and chokes or coughs, your dog could *benefit from being trained to stop pulling* through the use of a head halter or harness, that is specially designed to reduce pulling. Training is highly recommended. This requires time from a pet guardian, lots of repetition and patience.

Microchip vs Collars

The main reason dogs wear a collar is to carry ID tags with their pet owners' contact information and current rabies mandated vaccination tag in case your dog becomes lost. Your dog can also be stolen from your home and/or property or can be even be mistaken for an unwanted dog, where someone just keeps your dog. Having a microchip can offer some protection, if they become lost, the finder can bring the dog to a veterinarian clinic or shelter to have the dog scanned. This is why it's even a better reason to get your dog microchipped.

If your pet gets out often, you should consider buying a *dog tracker* online for your pet, as well as making sure all your home's windows, doors, gates and property fences are 100% secure. Your dog can get out by digging under your fence, or that you can be too low for your dog to easily jump over. Some dogs like to climb over taller fences and can slide in between the gates. Some dogs may even know how to open gates. In any case, collars can be taken off or ID tags can be lost. Microchips are underneath your dog's skin and they can't be easily removed. I recommend occasionally check your dog's microchip to make sure that the information is correct and that it can be read. I had two of my dog's microchips scan tested, to find out that, no information was reading. I wouldn't have known any other way. So, maybe next time you get an opportunity, have your dog microchip checked out!   Go the extra mile for your dog by verifying that it is properly working and that the contact information is correct.

Adoptable Dogs at the Shelter Video!

Chapter 2
Condition of Dogs at Intake and Dog Picture Stories

Puppy on the right was brought into Palm Beach County Animal Control by a police officer with a broken elbow and possibly needed an amputation. She urgently needed a foster and was on the urgent status to be put to sleep (PTS) list. I understand she was pulled out by a rescue.

This puppy was found emaciated due to severe neglect and was part of an investigation.

Neglected Caged Dog Story Video

On October 13, 2014, at 7:23 AM this sweet, shy, female brindle pit bull mix, was found in a dumpster, inside a garbage bag with bricks on top of her, so that she couldn't get out. Her story was covered by the news media.

Vonda

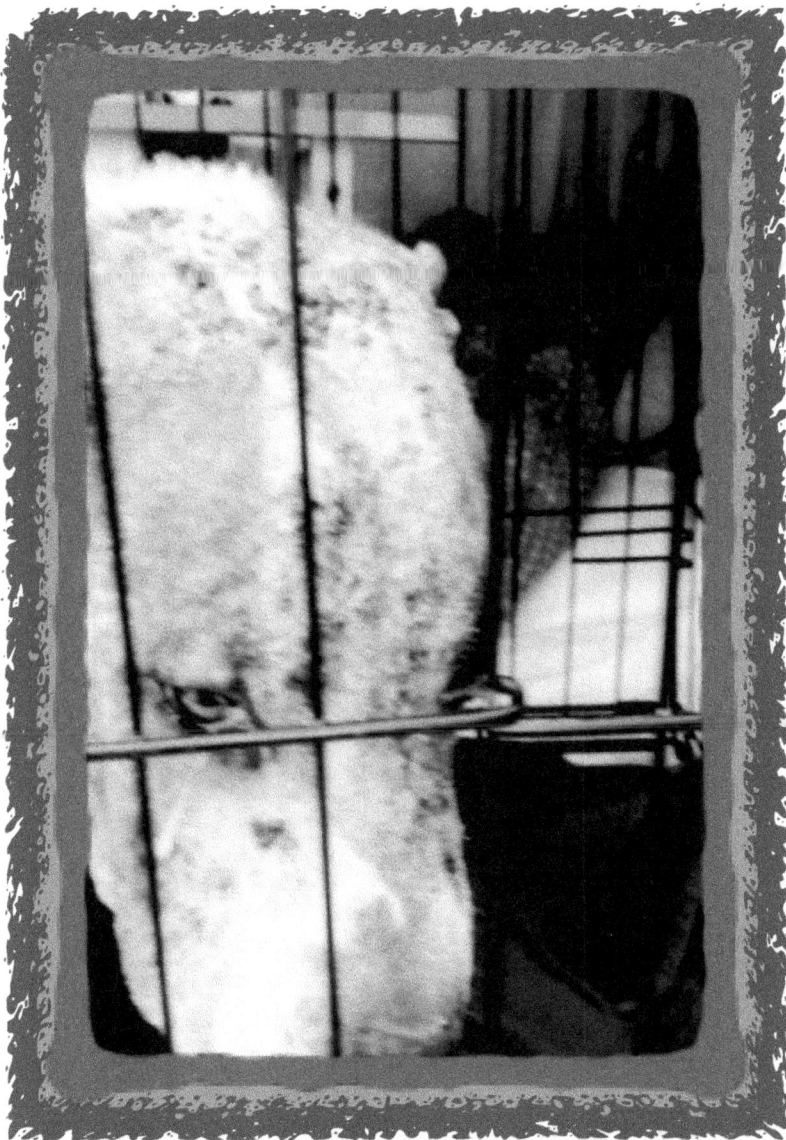

Vonda was found with severe Demodex, no hair on her body, and was in a lot of pain. She was rescued by a friend and was successfully adopted. Her name was changed to **Kanoa** in Hawaiian, the

meaning of the name is "The free one". They added a sibling dog to their family and they are living happily ever after.

Susie

ID #A1790100 - Black and white 5 year- old, 35 lb. mixed breed and crate trained. She was a staff favorite, great with children and had everything going for her. She had a foster at one point. Over time, life in the shelter made her anxious and she was not getting along with other dogs. She was put to sleep a couple of days after this picture was taken. RIP sweet beautiful little Susie.

Carol

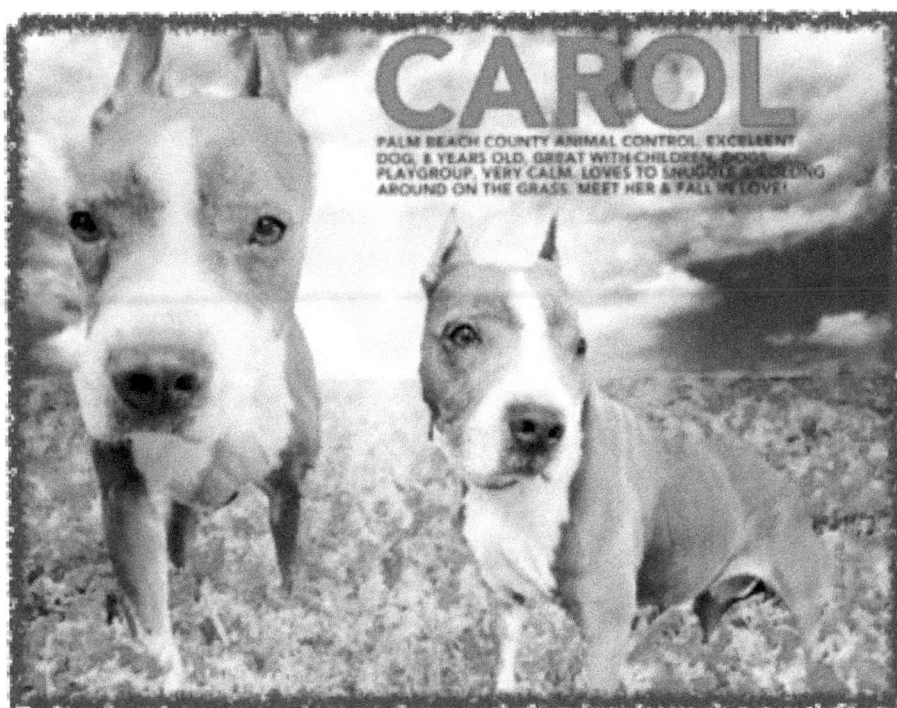

She was adopted! I occasionally get a-happy adoption picture from her family.

Kiki

ID #A1251256 - This 8 year old pit bull was found on 1/4/14 at Robbins Road. She was brought in and surrendered to Palm Beach County Animal Care and Control. A friend of mine fostered her when she came down with Canine Infectious Respiratory Disease (CIRD) aka Kennel cough dog cold. She was in the local shelter longer than any other dog. She got lucky and found temporary residence at

Peggy Adams Rescue League totaling for about 2 1/2 years or more. I saw her again on 12/15/15,when I took a video of her to promote her and tried to get her adopted. She was showing symptoms of getting sick and ended up with cancer. Shortly after she was not responding to treatment and she started to suffer. On her last day, she was fed hamburgers under a tree, surrounded by all of the staff that, loved her so much, and then she was put to sleep. Many tears were shed for Kiki. It was sad to think this beautiful dog had no one to love and take care of her.

This is one of my first pictures of Kiki. I edited it to promote her again and inserted this colorful backdrop landscape. As soon as, I posted this picture on social media, I found out about her crossing over to Rainbow Bridge. Here is to everyone that helped her out. RIP Kiki!

Last Time I Saw Kiki Adoption Video!

Dexter, Severe Demodex Video!

Christmas Day Adoption Video!

These beautiful pictures and the video above was taken on Christmas Day, 2015. Luke was very playful and just wanted love. RIP Luke.

The Christmas Rescue Signing Dogs Video!

Stagg

ID #A1717557 was a volunteer and staff favorite. This 2-year old gray pit mix was found on Avenida Ermosa in West Palm Beach, Florida. He was put to sleep on 2/21/14. RIP Stagg!

Toby was fostered out when he came down with CIRD - Kennel Cough. He got better and had to go back to the shelter to find a home on the adoption floor. The volunteers spent 3 months working hard to save him and to find him a home. We received a letter from the shelter saying he was unsafe, and that the decision had been made to put him to sleep on 3/22/16. RIP Toby.

Check out this video while he was still alive here:

Toby and Friends Adoption Video!

Pinky

I will never forget when I first saw Pinky, I fell in love
instantly. As a new volunteer at Palm Beach County
Animal Care and Control, I felt lost and
overwhelmed by all of the dogs in need in Kennel 1,
the main adoption floor with 50 kennels, almost all
the dogs were paired up with other dogs in there. I
thought how awesome it would be to make a
difference to at least one or a few of these dogs for

the day. Pinky was one of the first dogs I worked with at the shelter that, I had fallen in love with.

I volunteered every Sunday and I hardly ever saw other volunteers. Just a few occasional regulars that, I would very sometimes team up with. Many times there were no leashes available to walk the dogs. I was all alone, with easily 85 dogs, in the kennel. I was confused as, to which dog to choose to take for a walk and work with, they all need attention. Animal shelters are low budgeted and low staffed. Most of the County's budget goes to other city departments before they fund budgets for local community animal shelters. I felt discouraged and emotional to think that these dogs had no one or anything. One day I walked Pinky out far from the kennel area, for some quiet time, under a mango tree, where so we could enjoy our time and mango together, some quiet time and feel the fresh breeze. I then noticed she had a large open

wound on the left side of her face and neck, probably from another dog that had bitten her. If you look closely at her cover picture, you can see the wound on the left side.

Hence, to be fair to all the animals, the shelter must give the new dogs an equal opportunity to get adopted. This protocol moves the newer animal intakes to the adoption floor. Pinky ended up being euthanized. There was no more room for her and her time was up for adopters or fosters to save her. This was a very sad day for me. RIP Pinky, you where my favorite dog!

Smoke

SMOKE

A1807810 is a excellent 5y, housebro...
crate trained, good with other dogs.
Palm Beach County Animal Control.
Come meet him and fall in love!

www.everythingdogs.net

It was the Valentine season of 2016 when I met Smoke for his adoption promotion pictures and videos. He contracted kennel cough (CIRD), and was lucky to get a foster. With scars from side to side around his nose, cheeks and mouth from being forcefully tied hut, it was apparent he had been abused and had suffered pain. Once his treatment was finished, he was returned to the shelter to get on the adoption floor. Soon after, he went back on

urgent status. After a few months or so at the shelter, he was not doing well in the shelter environment. He was not doing well in the shelter envirnment. He was noted for having some behavioral issues. We found a rescue, but due to his behavior issues, the shelter did not allow the rescue to take him. This was when his foster family stepped up to adopt him.

Smoke's Adoption Valentine's Video!

Xoxo (pronounced Zozo)

Xoxo Spent over a year in the shelter and came out looking worse then when she went in. She had ear infections and her paws and the backs of her legs were red and raw from lying on the cold concrete. She is a unique looking dog that everyone just falls in love with (those ears, those curves, that bum!!!). Her foster mom says looks like a cross between a Tasmanian Devil and a potato. 😂😂😂 Xoxo is around 5 years old and weighs around 60 pounds in these pictures. She is good on a leash, does great in the car and is house trained! She absolutely loves people She loves to chew on toys but never furniture or things she shouldn't! She is extremely smart and knows sit, paw and stay most of the time. She is a sweet cuddly girl who is waiting for you to fall in love with her!!

XOXO Adoption Video!

Samantha

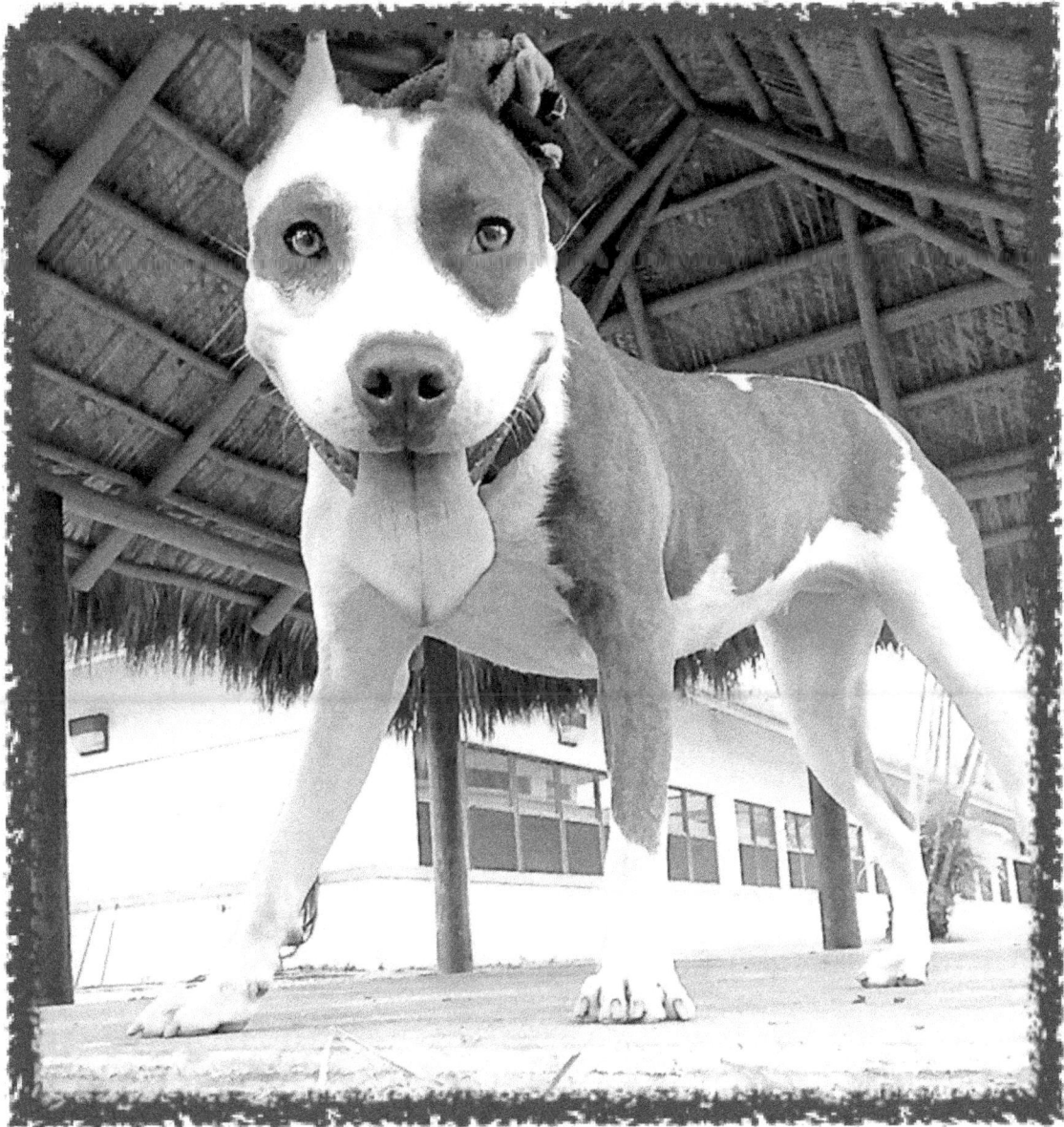

Samantha was fostered by a friend of mine when she had come down with Kennel-Cough (CIRD). She got better and after clearance from staff veterinarian, she was then return to get back on the adoption floor. After a while, we had received a call that Samantha was on the urgent status list again at the shelter again, with a 4-day notice to be put to sleep. I managed to pull all of our resources together and posted new videos of her urgently all over social media adoptable dog pages. Because she is a pitbull, there were no rescues that could take her at the time. Soon after, someone saw my video of her on a adoptable page on social media, and they came to adopt her with another dog named Rusty.

Two weeks later her adopter was packing to move out of town. Her existing older dog did not like the new dogs and had trouble accepting the new dogs in to the house. There was a fight by the existing dog, which triggered the owner to shoot and kill Rusty during the fight. A call was made to pick up Rusty's body and Samatha because they did not want her anymore. An officer went there to investigate. Samantha was in quarantine isolation for two to three weeks before we could start looking for a home again for her.

Samantha was finally successfully adopted and is now happily in her forever home!

Jazz and Shadow

Jazz and Shadow Happily Together Video!

One day while walking my dogs, I noticed we had a new neighbor. I was very impressed by how she handled her dogs when walking them. We later engaged in a conversation about her dogs. She told me that, one morning she had the urge to adopt a dog, so she went to the shelter and ended up adopting these two dogs, Jazz and Shadow. They were both on urgent status to be on the put to sleep list. Jazz was found in an abandoned apartment building and a Palm Beach County Animal Control officers retrieved her on sight for intake. She later caught kennel cough (CIRD). Shadow was owner surrendered because of "the size of the new apartment was too small" was noted. Shadow was very scared in the shelter environment. The head trainer and kennel manager at the time worked with them on basics training, that they both picked up on very quickly.

4th of July Fireworks

Brad Pit

Statistically, the day after 4th of July is the busiest day at shelters and the most common holiday for dogs to run off getting lost, resulting in getting hit by a car, or getting hurt in some way.

This is because, when dogs hear firework (gunshots or thunder too), their natural survival instinct is to panic and to run away from home. Some dogs develop noise phobias that, can cause them to want to hide or try to escape.

Please keep your pet safe inside your home during any fireworks in your area, and provide some comfort to your dogs.

Take extra steps to ensure all pet's safety.

Keep a close eye on your dog during the commotion and make sure your pet is wearing proper identification.

Firework Tips

Preparation - Expending your dog's excess energy, before the fireworks start by taking them on a long walk to tire her/him out to put your dog in a more calm state of mind. Then keep your dog in a familiar space where there won't be loud fireworks displays. A blacked out safe room (is ideal so that you're dogs, don't see the firework lights going off, that can crate excitement), some relaxing music (or even an action movie to blend in the sound effects) and aromatherapy an help.

Calming tips - If you find it necessary to use sedation medication prescribe by a veterinarian, you can also consider CBD tincture on their favorite treat and or a *"thundershirt"*, to calm your dog during the fireworks. A thundershirt is a wearable solution that can be used to help your pet with dog separation anxiety, travel stress, fear of thunder, other loud noises and other canine anxieties. Even a well fitted t-shirt can help. Lavender aromatherapy can really help to calm your dog!

Communication with your dog - While with your dog during the fireworks, sending a calming message that, they have nothing to worry about, will help your dog to relax. Keep in mind that humans communicate with words and dogs communicate with energy. They will look to their pack leader for clues on how they should behave. If you're not making it a big deal or showing a lot of excitement about the fireworks, then they will learn to be less concerned as well.

Brad Pit's Story

Brad Pit's Time with me and Adoption Video!

It was during the July 4th holiday, when someone came to my front gate at my home with this beautiful gray pitbull mix dog that, they found a stray. I took him to the shelter because I could not find a rescue to take him. I was currently fostering a momma dog and her 9 puppies, plus my dogs.

I thought I could help find him a home by promoting him with flyers and videos I made of him while he was at Palm Beach County Animal Care and Control shelter, as an active foster, and volunteer. I thought he was so handsome. I called him Brad Pitt.

The shelter neutered him while they were at full capacity, as they usually are during the hot summer holidays. Many of the staff, trainers and volunteers were on vacation for the holiday. Time was running out for Brad Pitt. I felt so horrible for taking him there. I though I developed a good relationship with the shelter after my few years of helping out in so many ways. There was no success in introducing him to other dogs, in the attempt of pairing him up with other kennel mates, by the volunteers because, most of the staff trainers where out on summer vacation. It did not go well the two times that they tried. They could not keep him or get him adopted out in the short time he had there. I posted him all over social media on adoptable pages, in hope of finding him an awesome safe home. I cried for a week when he was put to sleep. I still have an open wound that I carry till this very day. I truly believe he could have been with a great family today. If we only had more rescues taking pit bull breeds, more fosters and more dogs sterilization programs, he could still be with us. RIP Brad Pitt. I loved you and I am so sorry!

Check out his video, so you can see how he loved the sweet potato treats I brought for him and how special our time was together.

Puppy Mill Dogs

Almost all dogs sold at puppy stores are puppy mill pets. We should be concerned with the selling of puppies commercially, as breeders are capitalizing on the sale of them, making as much money as possible with as little overhead.

Every year in America, it's estimated that 2.11 million puppies that are sold originate from puppy mills. While 5 million are killed in sheeters because they are at full capacity and there are not enough adoptions.

Here is how you can make a difference:
- Act as a publicist for your local animal shelter to encourage your community to adopt shelter pets.

- Sign up for volunteering and or fostering.

Cons of Puppy Mills Designer Dogs

- Dogs can spend most of their lives in cramped cages with no room to play or exercise.

- Often, the water and food provided for the puppies an contaminated and crawling with bugs.

- Puppies can even be often malnourished.

- There is no way to verify if the owner or the store manager says that they are not breading dogs.

- They can have psychological problems. With limited, no regulations, or enforcement, puppy mills have no cleanup control. This means that dogs can be living in urine and feces for indefinite periods.

- Puppies in mills are sometimes found with bleeding or swollen paws and feet from falling through the wire cages, severe tooth decay, ear infections, dehydration and lesions on their eyes which often can lead to blindness.

- Most puppy mills have no veterinary care, climate control or protection for the animals from the heat, cold, rain or snow.

- It's common to find dogs in puppy mills with collars that have been fastened so tightly that they become embedded into the dog's neck.

- Female dogs are bred at every opportunity, with little to no recovery time in between litters. Then after a few years, they are physically depleted to the point that they can no longer reproduce. Breeding females are often killed.

• It costs taxpayers more with the needed enforcement of cleaning, sheltering, resources, rehabilitations, pick-ups and euthanasias of sick animals.

• No verification screening adoption application.

• Again, there are about 5 million dogs and cats being put to sleep in shelters.

• They receive minimal, if any, veterinary care and inbreeding is a common practice. Disease, genetic disorders, and heartworms are the norms. The breeding females produce one litter after another in cramped cages with no concern for their health.

• Puppy mill dogs are sold to pet stores and advertised on the internet and in newspapers. If you are told that a breeding facility is "USDA-licensed" or "USDA-inspected", this only means that minimal standards of food, water and shelter have been met. It says nothing about meeting the needs or securing the welfare of the breeder's dogs. AKC registration papers and also mentions nothing about the condition of the dog, or how it was raised.

- Cruel breeding
- More expensive
- Don't pay tax
- Designer dogs
- Health issues
- Inhumane conditions

Reputable breeders want you to visit their facility.

Shelter vs Rescues

Shelter Adopt a Dog Mouth Promotion Video!

There is a difference between a community service animal control shelter and a private charity organization. Community shelters have to take in all the dogs and cats that come into the shelter, no matter what condition they come in. A private charity organization can pick and choose which animal can be brought to them.

As a community, we can work together towards:

- Strengthening Anti-Cruelty Laws and related penalties.
- Fighting puppy mills.
- Enacting strong Cost of Care laws for seized animals caught up in legal cases.
- Putting a stop to animal fighting, including dog and cock-fighting.
- Supporting the creation and the expansion of subsidized no-cost or low-cost spay/neuter programs.

Emergency Hurricane Shelter Videos

During Huricane Erma Window View

Getting Crates Safe & Ready to Ship Dogs From Hurricane Erma to Get Adopted!

After Math of Hurricane Erma - Palm Beach County Animal Control

Adopable Shelter Dogs Video!

Coda

Coda had a server case of Demodex; he had no hair, in pain, red and irritated. He was treated with IV's GTS Husky Rescue. In this picture below he has new hair growth!

Just one unaltered female dog
could reproduce an average of 6-10
puppies per litter and can
reproduce up to 2 times per year.
6 X 2 = 12 per year alone.

One unaltered female dog and her
offspring can reproduce 67,000
puppies in only six years.

If her puppies are left unaltered,
they could reproduce the same.
That adds up quickly.
Within the seven years.

One female cat and her offspring
can reproduce an incredible
370,000 kittens.

Lucky

This husky just had his eye removed. He then lost his vision in the other eye too because his previous owner did not give him eye drops. He was in a lot of pain. As soon as he had his surgery, he had a smile back on his face. He got adopted by a volunteer. GTS Husky Rescue.

Puppy Bowl Adoption Event Video!

This was an Amber Animal Outreach event. The founder started the rescue at 12 years old. She was homeschooled and is very influential in the animal community, helping animals in all conditions and raising lots of money for them.

Chapter 3
How we are Bringing our Euthanasia Numbers Down

Unsterilized Animal Chart

Together, we can save the lives of all adoptable pets in Palm Beach County with "Countdown to Zero" to bring animal welfare organizations to end the euthanasia for adoptable animals in Palm Beach County. This is a 10-year sterilization spay/neuter plan. A public-private community collaboration, initiated by Palm Beach County Animal Care and Control, the Board of County Commissioners and Peggy Adams Animal Rescue League.

They believe that our community has the expertise, the means and the obligation to aggressively implement strategies that, will reduce the number of animals needing temporary shelter and end the euthanasia of adoptable animals altogether in Palm Beach County.

At all times and in every way, we are advocates for animals. They ensure their safety and comfort, strive to alleviate their suffering and work to place and keep them in homes that, provide a responsible lifetime commitment for them. They speak out publicly to promote and defend their interests, and oppose all forms of animal cruelty. They promote spay/neuter and other critical programs focused on our goal of preventing the euthanasia of adoptable animals in Palm Beach County by 2024. They oppose taking the lives of healthy or treatable animals. They also provide services that promote responsible pet ownership and humane attitudes toward all life because they understand the critical role people play in improving the welfare of animals in our community.

Check out this video that I put together with some important animal statistics; to bring animal awareness to County Commissioners on the need to help animals in our community by approving a budget to control the animal population numbers. This can put an end to euthanasia for the masses of healthy adoptable animals that are being put to sleep every day.

Everything Dogs Series Introduction Video

Shelter Adoptable Cats Video!

This Palm Beach County Animal Control Alumni, smiling dog, was adopted at the event!
Happy Dance!

Sterilization and Animal Population

My Fosters Momma Oreo & Her 9 Puppies Video!

Mom Dog Trying to Get Away From Puppy Feeding Video!

Momma Oreo was found tied to a pole in a park in Belle Glade, Florida. This picture shows her with her 2nd litter of 9 puppies that I fostered when they came down with kennel cough (CIRD)

What Happens if We Don't Sterilize!

Their is a serious issue with animal over population everywhere. It is costing millions of communities tax dollars to euthanize millions of healthy good dogs and cats. Spaying and neutering can bring down the high number of euthanasia in shelters down fast. Unfortunately, about 75% of animals generally will be euthanized.

Please spay/neuter your pet. There are also so many health benefits too! Spaying helps prevent uterine infections and breast cancer which is fatal in about 50 percent of dogs and 90 percent of cats.

Spaying your pet before her first heat offers the best protection from these diseases. Neutering provides major health benefits for high energy dogs that stray from home.

This is Reba at only 8 months old here, she is pregnant expecting puppies. She was Rescue from Palm Beach County Animal Care & Control by Blessed Paws. Reba Being Rescued Video!

Around the Clock Spay/ Neuter Marathon

These pictures are of the first morning of this event, before the cats were brought in to the room sterilization. Some of the cats were already pregnant, but they all did great while recovering after surgery.

Op Around the Clock Marathon In Action Video!

"OP (Operation) Around the Clock" was sponsored by Darbster's Foundation. Thanks to the help of community volunteers, 491 cats were sterilized in February 2013. We trapped and released over 600 cats. Darbster's Vegan Bistro is located on the Lake Worth, Florida. waterfront. All the proceeds from Darbster's food are donated to help the animals in our community. In 2013 and 2014, they donated $10,000 for "Op Around the

Clock Spay/Neuter Marathon". In conjunction with Palm Beach County Animal Care and Control, Darbster's continues helping animals and saving many animal's lives in our community.

Animals are not allowed inside county government buildings and offices, but community cats living outdoors on county-owned property can be cared for by employees. Animal Care and Control helps with trapping efforts. The cats are sterilized, microchipped, ear clipped, vaccinated and then they are returned and released to their original site.

Animal Care and Control's Working Cats program, allows local businesses the opportunity to bring a homeless cat into the workplace free of charge. Selected working cats are healthy, friendly and well-adjusted. Their presence can bring a sense of calm to a hectic setting and can help to reduce employee

stress. Having a cat as a company mascot may help customers remember the business's name, or give them an extra reason to stop in.

As a community, we can work together towards:

- Strengthening Anti-Cruelty Laws and related penalties.

- Fighting puppy mills.

- Enacting strong Cost of Care laws for seized animals caught up in legal cases.

- Putting a stop to animal fighting, i n c l u d i n g dogfighting and cockfighting.

My Ralph

- Supporting the creation and the expansion of subsidized no-cost or low-cost spay/neuter programs.

- Abandoned and homeless cats live among us in all geographical areas. By trapping, sterilizing, microchipping, vaccinating and then returning the animals to the property, this problem is then humanely addressed.

It's a common goal for shelters across the United State to become no kill shelters by 2025!

Chapter 4
Animal Euthanasia

Animal euthanasia (euthanasia from Greek: εὐθανασία; "good death") it is the act of putting an animal to death or allowing it to die by withholding extreme medical measures. Reasons for euthanasia include incurable and especially painful conditions or diseases, lack of resources to continue supporting the animal or questionable laboratory test procedures. Euthanasia methods are designed to cause minimal pain and distress. Euthanasia is distinct from animal slaughter and pest control, although in some cases the procedure is the same.

1. Be painless
2. Achieve rapid unconsciousness followed by death
3. Minimize animal fear and distress
4. Be reliable and irreversible

Acceptable Euthanasias
Intravenous Anesthetic Injection

This is the best practice recommended for being *the most rapid-acting.* Unconsciousness, respiratory failure, then followed rapidly by cardiac arrest within 30 seconds. Observers generally describe the method as leading to a quick and peaceful death.

Some veterinarians perform a two-stage process: an initial injection, that simply renders the pet unconscious and a second injection that causes death.

This allows the owner the chance to say goodbye to a living pet without their emotions stressing out their pet. It also greatly mitigates any tendency toward spasm and other involuntary movements, which tends to increase the emotional upset that, the pet's owner experiences.

Intraperitoneal (IP) Injection of 20% Pentobarbitone Solution

Urgent Dogs - Palm Beach County at Animal Care & Control Palm Beach County September 29, 2014 · West Palm Beach, West Palm Beach

RIP - Euthanized -No Owner/No Rescues/ No Adopter! I'm so sorry we failed you. **URGENT FOSTER NEEDED** KENNEL COUGH/ CIRD
AVAILABLE FOR ADOPTION - ABEE
Animal ID Intake Date 9/13/2014 A1748973, Color: Chocolate, Female Unsterilized, 9 months, Large, 54 lbs.

- Slow acting. Takes longer to take effect than an IV injection: 15-30 minutes.
- A larger dose may be required when given intravenously.
- May be used when collapsed or poor venous access precludes the IV injection.
- May not be suitable for the euthanasia of larger animals.
- The use of pre-euthanasia drugs may prolong the time until death.
- May cause irritation to the peritoneum, particularly with concentrations >20%.
- It can be combined with a local anesthetic to reduce the risk of irritation.
- The animal may become distressed when it starts to lose consciousness.
- Maybe a practical alternative when the IV injection is difficult for fractious, stray or feral cats and neonatal kittens and puppies. It is advisable to return cats to a secure cage after injection. They may become distressed while the drug takes effect.

Intravenous IV Injection of Anaesthetic Agents, (given as an overdose) - Thiopentone or Propofol; Thiobarbiturate or Phenol Base Compound

• Rapid-acting

• Rapid loss of consciousness

•It may be suitable if animals are already anesthetized for surgery and on humane grounds, not permitted them to regain consciousness.

• Relatively large volumes or high concentrations are required to euthanize animals. Potentially making it impractical for routine use depending upon the commercial availability of the preparation.

• Underdosing may lead to recovery

• May be used in combination with a pre-euthanasia drug, if required.

• Requires training

• Costs may preclude routine use

• There are many other conditional and acceptable ways.

Intravenous (IV) Intracardiac (IC) Injection of Potassium Chloride (KCl) after General Anesthesia

- Rapid-acting
- Causes death by cardiac arrest
- It should never be used without prior general anesthesia to achieve sufficient insensibility and analgesia. This blocks the painful side effects of this method.

Intravenous (IV) or Intracardiac (IC) Injection of Magnesium Sulphate (MgSO4) after General Anesthesia

- Rapid-acting
- Causes death by cardiac arrest
- It should never be used without prior general anesthesia, to achieve sufficient insensibility and analgesia, to block the painful side effects.

- Requires training to ensure that, the operator can assess the suitability of anesthetic depth prior to use.
- Large volumes are required for euthanasia.
- A saturated solution is required, but this makes the liquid very viscous and can result in difficulty in administration.

Inhalation of Gaseous Anesthetics - Halothane, Enflurane, Isoflurane and Sevoflurane

- Slow acting
- It requires high concentrations to be effective.
- Only suitable for small animals (weighing <7kg)
- It may be suitable if animals are already anesthetized for surgery, on humane grounds, and not permitted to regain consciousness.
- Difficult to administer to large animals
- In un-anesthetized animals, the smell of the volatile agent may be unpleasant. They may try to avoid it, or hold their breath for a short time.

- In un-anesthetized animals, it may cause respiratory distress as it may act as an irritant.
- It can be harmful to operators: risk of narcosis if exposed to the volatile agent.
- Expensive
- Not routinely recommended, as there are better alternatives

Death by Stabbing of the Heart Stick

Still acceptable by the Humane Society of the United States (HSUS), cats and dogs are awake without sedation. They are usually muzzled while someone holds them down. Only more aggressive dogs get a sedative. When blue juice, commonly known as food coloring, is added to a barbiturate poisonousness anesthetic injection called **sodium pentobarbital** that causes the death. In the veterinary world it is called **euthanyl,** and if you have ever had a pet "put to sleep", it was likely with this blue-colored anesthetic being injected into the veins. Veterinarians are fortunate to be able to humanely end an animal's life. However, many performing this procedure are not properly trained. This often results in multiple attempts to get it straight into the heart while someone restrains the animal. This is very barbaric, often in the first attempt can be difficult to find the heart. This results in a very cruel and painful death.

This is done by a stabbing jab of the poison, with a stick link syringe, that has to go through the chest wall forcing its way between the chest muscles and nerves. If not done right, they have to force it back in again to attempt to get it in the heart. It is not ensured that it will get to their heart in the first attempt.

When in the heart, they can feel the syringe pulsate from the heart. The dead animals are then thrown in a bag and then put in a barrel with others. It has been reported that animals don't often die right away, and are put in a freezer left to suffer and die without any pain killers.

Gas Chamber

Rarely, it's not just one dog at a time put into the gas chamber. Usually, it's from 5 to 15 and more at a time. This is not a humane death. The dogs tend to urinate and defecate on themselves as the poison gets into their little bodies. One can hear the cries and howls as they suffocate. It takes some time before the dogs are killed. This allows the dogs to become very frightened and anxious. They struggle very hard to get out to survive. However, it is somewhat common for dogs to survive this terrifying gas chamber. Of course, they suffer major damage. Usually if they survive, they are just put back in again. This form of euthanasia is more common than you may think!

Commercially manufactured chamber using compressed cylinder CO_2 may be acceptable for certain wildlife species. CO_2 is produced from dry ice or generated from any other method is condemned.

Carbon Monoxide

CO must be provided by a compressed cylinder. It is used only in a chamber that has been commercially manufactured for CO euthanasia and is to be properly maintained. The chamber must be designed to minimize stress and to allow for the appropriate separation of animals. Chambers must never be overcrowded.

CO is a hazardous substance, considered especially dangerous because it is odorless, tasteless, colorless and explosive. Repeated exposure to CO, even at low levels, can result in many serious long-term effects including (but not limited to); cancer, infertility, and heart disease. CO chambers must, therefore, be used with extreme caution. Proper guidelines must be in place to ensure both the humane death for the animals, and the safety of personnel.

Carbon Dioxide

Carbon dioxide (CO_2) is not acceptable for routine use in animal care and control facilities for the euthanasia of companion animals. However commercially manufactured chambers, using a compressed cylinder CO2 may be acceptable for certain wildlife species. CO2 produced from dry ice or generated from any other method is condemned.

Decompression Chamber

A decompression chamber is a spinning mechanical unit, which houses small cages, were animals are enclosed. The spinning of the unit prevents the animals from breathing; causing them to lose consciousness and eventually die. Today this method is considered inhumane under the American Veterinary Medical Association. Also, know as AVMA guidelines.

Electrocution

This method is for small animals, such as dogs and cats. This sometimes involves putting a metal clip on the animal's lip and inserting a metal rectal electrocution probe. This method was described to us several years ago by a well-known large humane shelter director. However, in my research, I did not find it currently listed in the AVMA guidelines.

What Happens to the Dead Bodies of Animals Killed in Shelters?

Each facility handles this problem differently. In some communities, the bodies are simply stored to ultimately be buried. In larger communities or those with more particular regulations, the bodies are kept frozen until removed from the facility.

The disposal procedures we know of include:

Cremation

This is the most expensive method used. It is not considered typical due to the expense.

Rendering Plant

This is the least expensive since truckers normally pick up the bodies for no fee. The truckers get their payment from the rendering plants where the bodies are brought. The rendering plants get their monies from the products they produce (tallow, meat and blood byproducts, hair byproducts). They are included in everyday products, that we purchase, to use for ourselves and for our animals. To determine which products contain these rendering plant products, read the labels and look for terms such as; **hydrolyzed animal protein, blood meal, bone meal, meat byproducts, tallow, etc.**

Note that not all rendering plants choose to dispose of household pets in this way. It all depends on the rendering plant. If your local plant does, please understand that such a plant is providing a community service.

Burial in Landfills

This is not allowed in some areas, but it is a common disposal method around the United States.

Chapter 5
High-Risk Animals

High rise animals cats, square heads, American pit bulls, German Shepherds, Big or Black Dog Syndrome (BDS or BBD) are all disputed phenomenons. Black dogs are passed over for adoption in favor of lighter-colored animals. Animal shelters often use this term of BBD, the type of larger dark-colored mixed-breed, said to be typically passed by with adopters.

Tank

This chapter is especially dedicated to Tank, in his loving memory. Animal ID #A1734677 from Palm

Beach County Animal Care and Control. You were so special to me RIP Tank! He is my cover boy for this chapter.

Tank's Time with me Adoption Video!

In this adoption video you get to see Tank; being well behaved, eating sweet potatoes, getting his tummy rubbed and what our time together was like. Unfortunately a couple of days later, without a foster notification for someone to foster him, he was put to sleep. They said he was not doing well in the shelter environment and started reacting. This is not necessarily true. The truth is that if the city had a raise and improve the budget for shelters to afford more staff, more trained animal enrichment coordinators and more enforced sterilization programs. Putting a dog to sleep should be something of the past. RIP sweet Tank.

Research has identified geographic locations, fear of stigma against certain breed types, and the fact that large black dogs are often portrayed as aggressive in films and on television correlates.

Initial research experience has shown that when people are viewing shelter dogs walking through the adoption floor or video-recording visitors, that they all spent equal amounts of time looking at every dog, regardless of the coat color. Other studies have suggested brindle dogs may be more likely to experience longer delays before adoption than black dogs. Coat color bias seems evident but may change depending on geographic location.

Black animals predominantly do not photograph as well as lighter-colored dogs. Lighter colored pets have an advantage with potential adopters browsing the site.

History

The issue has been gaining media attention since the mid 2000's. Tamara Delaney, an early activist against black dog syndrome, developed a website called Black Pearl Dogs in 2004, specifically to address this issue by educating the public. Black cats are similarly reported to be subject to the same phenomenon; with the added stigma of superstition and association with witchcraft. Some United State cities prohibit adoption of black cats around Halloween "for fear the felines would be used as holiday props or worse, as sacrifices for those who practice witchcraft." Wilipeda

Cats are the Highest Risk at Shelters

Pinta

ID # A1707355, 12/15/13, German Shepard mix.

Lady

ID #A175910 was in the foster program. By special request, I took these beautiful pictures. She is a very good girl. Happily adopted!

John on top ID #A1805468, K1-139, American pitbull, male 13 months old. Juno, Knight, Soldier, Prima (in the middle row) and no name dog, Prima (Adopted) and Hemi. All these dogs in this chapter are alumni

Blackie - ID# A1718637
Froggy

ID #A1715116 - ID # A170098 lab mix male, an intake on February 2011. Was found in Lantana, Florida. He was adopted on 4/10/14, then was brought back to the same shelter. He was a ball of energy. He knew not to pull the leash, stop, sit, stay and loved treats. You could easily get his attention. He responded very well. At one point he was fostered and then went back on the adoption floor. He enjoyed getting your attention by showing off how fast he could run to impress you. He was an amazing, good boy and a very impressive dog. He was euthanized. RIP Froggy, you were so special to me!

Puppie Happy Adoption Dance!

Hemi

ADOPT A BLACK DOG

Eddie

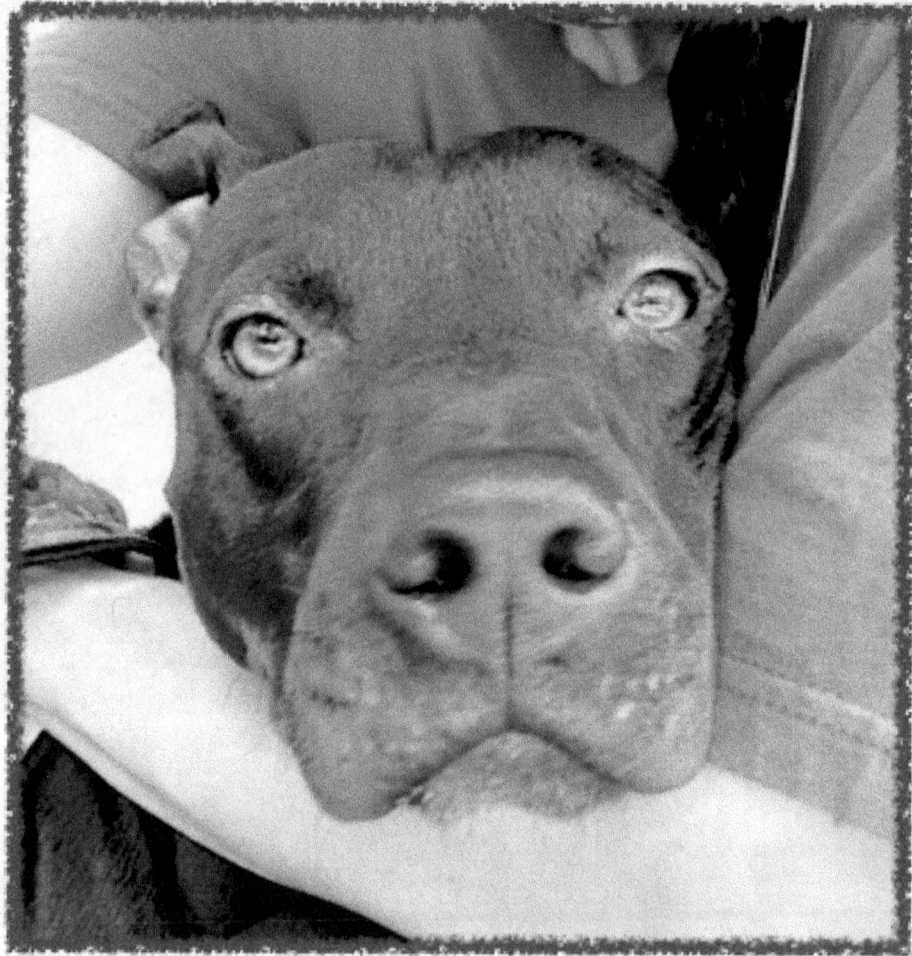

May 4, 2014 this dog was very sad when I was with him. He just had his head down low and wanted me to hold him. As if he had given up and wanted to get out of the shelter. I will never forget this day with him. He was put to sleep a couple of days after I took this picture. RIP sweet Eddie! You are in my heart forever!

Juno
My Foster Failure!
Rescued with CRID at 1 week
old with mom and 8 other
siblings.

Bandit

K 1 - 1 4 0 unaltered, 8 months old, 45 lbs., good with other dogs.

Adorable Black Dog at Adoption Event Video!

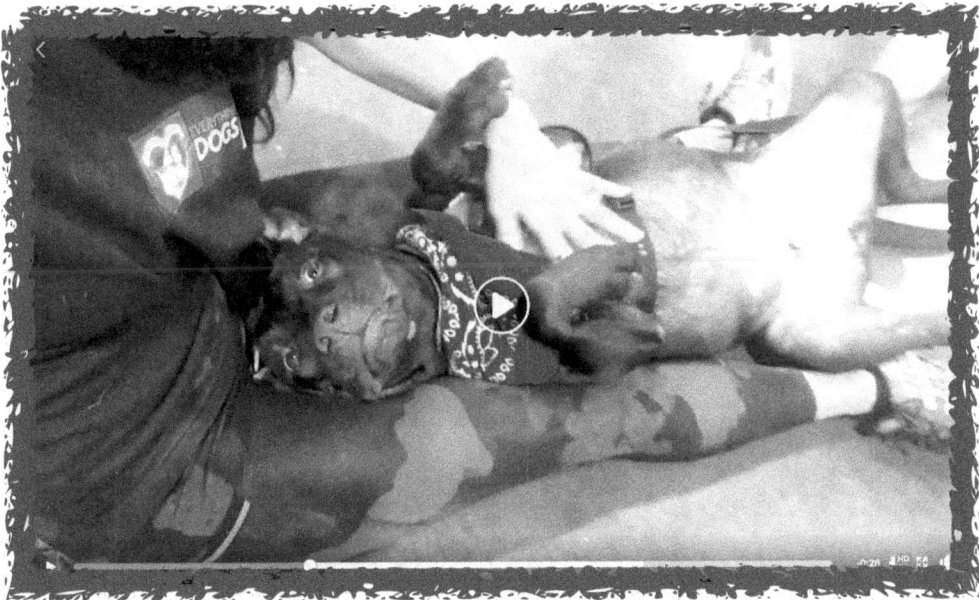

Martin

Briana's Adoption Video!

Onyx and Duke

Look at These sweet brothers with Ambers Animal
Outreach. 1-year-old German Shepherds mix

Onyx & Duke at an Adoption Event

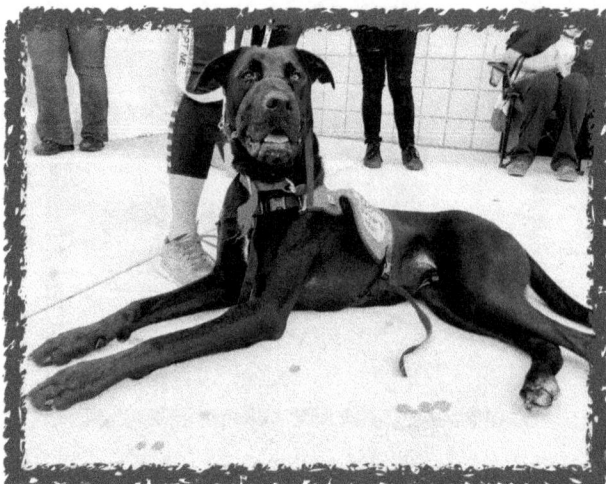

Beisha Adoption Video!

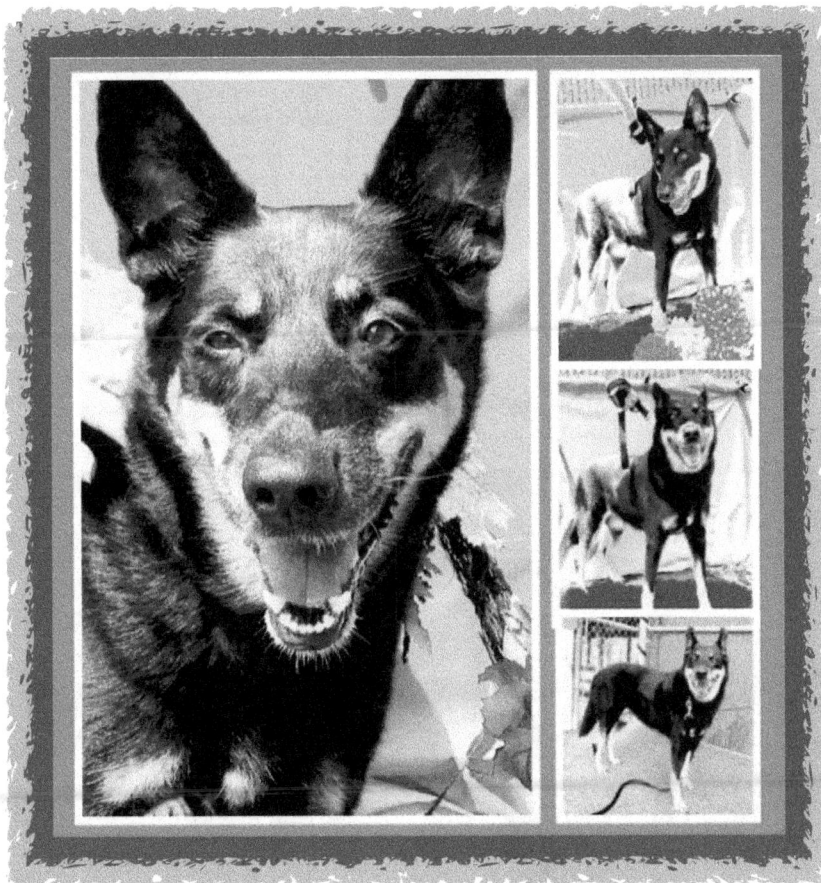

ID #A1661031 and ID #A1661031, 10 years old, good with other dogs. Her owner went into an assisted sliving facility and could not find anyone for her. Beisha spent several month at the shelter before she got adopted. And when she was, she was returned the next day because she wanted to say hello to another dog and her new guardian could not manage her well. She got back on the adoption floor, after a week on hold in quarantine. She then got adopted a couple of weeks after. When I took her out she would look for her owner.

Icee's Adoption Video!

ICEE
ID #A1933033

8 months old, ale, excellent with other dogs, very sweet & smart. Loves to play in water. Palm Beach County Animal Control. Come meet him & fall in love! Please SHARE

Thelma

Facebook Live, CBS Channel 12's Pet of the Day!

BRODY

3 years old, black/white, male, very affectionate & smart, A1927305. Excellent with other dogs. Come meet him & fall in love at Palm Beach County Animal Care & Control

Adopt a Black or Brindle Dog!

Chapter 6
Kennel-Mates Save Lives

GREG

Greg's Adoption Promotion Video!

Dogs that come into the shelter system are under a lot of stress. They are in a strange place and likely getting a new kennel mate. For so many dogs, it's a difficult situation. Adopting a pet is a responsibility for your pets full term of life.

Greg

ID #A17381553 K1-112 American Pitbull Terrier, neutered, 5 years old male. He was a shelter staff favorite for a long time. He had a total of **12 Kennel roommates** before he got adopted furever! With his excellent temperament, we were able to pair him up with many other dogs as kennel roommates. This is how we were able to buy more time for him.

While I was taking pictures of him playing with his roommate, a family saw him in action and adopted him! We were all so excited! We said our goodbyes and even applauded him, as we made an announcement on the shelters speakers that, "Greg was leaving the building". Unfortunately, he was returned less than 2 weeks later. The staff members were overwhelmingly sad for Greg. Good thing shortly thereafter, he was finally adopted for life. He lives with a family and has his own room and pajamas too!

Cranberry and Sauce

Cranberry, ID #A1706982, pitbull, spayed female, 8 months; she loves to play and sits on command. She was adopted. She came in with **Sauce,** ID # A1720378, pitbull, 2 years old, very calm temperament which got him adopted. However, the following week after taking these pictures, I saw noted that Sauce was put to sleep for non-specific behavior issues. Cranberry will miss him very much. RIP Sauce! We love you!

Critter and Lea

 **Critter,** ID #A1791687, male, white, 2 years old, housebroken, good with other dogs, cats and children. Got adopted!

 **Lea,** ID #A179533, tan and white female, 2 years old, housebroken, good with other dogs and children.

Abigail and Faith

Coco and Bella

Coco, ID #A1738985, Labrador retriever, female, 2 years old. Bella, ID #A1738453, American bulldog, female, 2 years old and. Both adopted!

Sugar and Hero Chloe

Sugar - ID #A1766256, spayed, female, 6 Years, 64 lbs. came in on 3/11/14, very sweet, sits, lays down and plays frisbee! She has excellent temperament. She was fostered when she came down with kennel Cough - CIRD by a friend of mine. Her cough went away and I think she was pulled out by a local rescue.

Chloe - ID #A154533 - Chloe is a hero. Her home was on fire while her family was sleeping. She woke her family up in the nick of time to save their lives. Unfortunately, they lost their home and her family couldn't find anyone or rescue. She got adopted!

CHARRO & BUDDY

Best roommates

Reme and Abby

Reme, ID #A1676510, 2/24/14, Plot Hound, white on nose, loves playing and to get attention. Very affectionate. In the same kennel with, Abby ID #A1719407, Plot Hound, female, shy sweet heart.

Jordan and Blacky

Jordon,   ID #A174747,
            9/4/2014, 2 years and 4 months old.
        Blacky - ID #A1727277, loves Jordon.

Quint and Eddie

Roommates

Radish and Chance

Radish ID #A1741453, pitbull, female, 2 years old.

Chance, ID #A1750201,   pitbull, 3 years old.
Got adopted. Happy dance!
Simba - ID #1695407, male lab mix and
Rocco - ID #1695512, male, mix pitbull.

TIko and Butch

Tiko - ID #A1379278, Golden retriever mix, neutered, 6 years old. Butch - ID #A1732297 German Shepherd mix, 8 years old, great on the leash. Awesome dogs in K1-148.

Loca and Farrah

Loca, ID #A1720967, pitbull mix, 2 years old. She is ready to run, play and pose for a pictures any time. She loves treats and can get on 2 legs to show you that, she can dance. She will carefully take a treat from you. Her kennel-mate was Farrah, ID #A1721152, is a Treeing Cur, female, 3 years old. She did not look good on that Sunday, so I had to take her to the clinic. She is beautiful, with a stunning with unique tan silver coat and light beautiful eyes. She was very sweet, loves to stretch and roll around. She came down with kennel cough (CIRD).

Loca A1720967

Bandit and Shadow

Bandit - K1-140, Just got on the adoption floor. No detailed information. Unaltered male, 8 months, 45 lbs. and **Shadow,** ID #A179087, 2-year-old, neutered on the right - male, 53 lbs.

Chapter 7
Fostering Urgent Dogs

Facebook Live, Pre-Filming of CBS Channel 12's "Pet of the Day" Video!

Usually, dogs that urgently need fosters have Canine Infection Respiratory Disease (CIRD). It is also known as Kennel Cough. It is highly contagious and transmitted through the air to other dogs. The dog may experience discomfort in the throat from irritation, runny nose and eyes, dry coughing, fever, decreased appetite, lack of energy and hacking. These are common side effects similar to a human's common cold that needs attention.

If you come in contact with a dog that, has CIRD, kennel cough you should immediately change, wash your clothing and disinfect the bottom of your shoes. If you have long hair, pick it up (to keep it from getting infected), or even wash it. Make sure you keep from spreading before coming in contact with other dogs. The Bordetella shot can help prevent cross-contamination from other dogs. Consult your veterinarian for information about this.

Shelter Foster Programs provide supplies, crates, food, and medicine. The foster term is short in length, 1 to 2 weeks. The house veterinarian must release them with a clean bill of health so that, they can go back on the adoption floor. If you have other dogs in the home, they should have the Bordetella shot to avoid contamination. Especially if your pet has not been exposed to it before. CIRD is not transmittable to cats. Infected dogs can be kept in a garage, porch or spare room.

When it is discovered that, a dog has CIRD the dog is pulled immediately from the adoption floor, to avoid contamination to the other dogs. They are moved to an isolated room where they have no visibility to the public. At this point, the infected dogs detailed information with status notices is emailed to qualified foster groups and rescues. They might have 24 to 48 hours, to get them out before it's too late. Every situation is different, as space is limited for incoming dogs. This list is updated throughout the day.

Ending a dogs' or cats' life, by injection to put them to sleep is not a peaceful experience. Putting them to "sleep" is far from the truth. It's no different than ending an animal's life by hanging or shooting, it just looks prettier and is more convenient. It cost money to our community and these animals should be with a family that, loves them. It still gives the same result of a forced violent death. In my opinion, the breeders who do not sterilize their animals are largely at fault for the overpopulation and the millions of dogs and

cats that are terminated.

It's very common when a dog ends up in a shelter to quickly become sick, or perhaps come in already sick with CIRD-Kennel Cough and/or have heartworms. Proper care of your pets and vaccinations can prevent disease.

Farrah

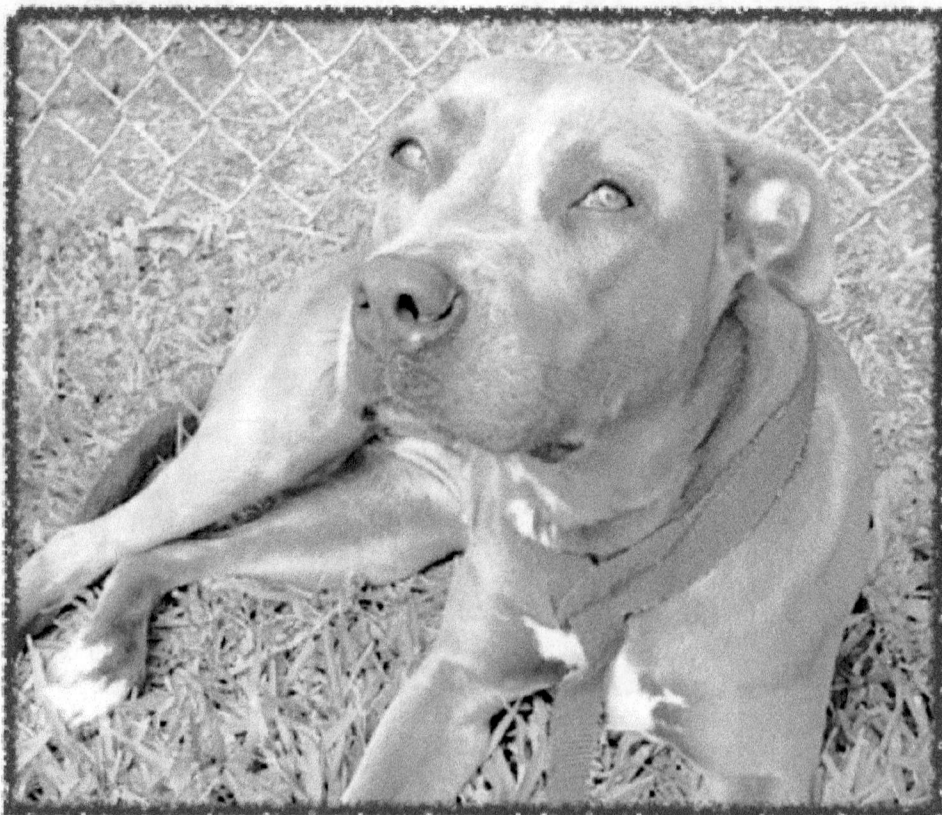

Farrah ID #A1721152 is listed as a Treeing Cur, female, 3 years old. She did not look too good when I took her out on that Sunday and spent some time with her. I then called to get her into the clinic for a checkup. She had CIRD as her immune system was low because of the stressful environment of the shelter. She had a beautiful stunning silver-gold coat and light eyes. She is a sweetheart that loves to stretch out and roll around.

Christmas Eve Dogs
2014

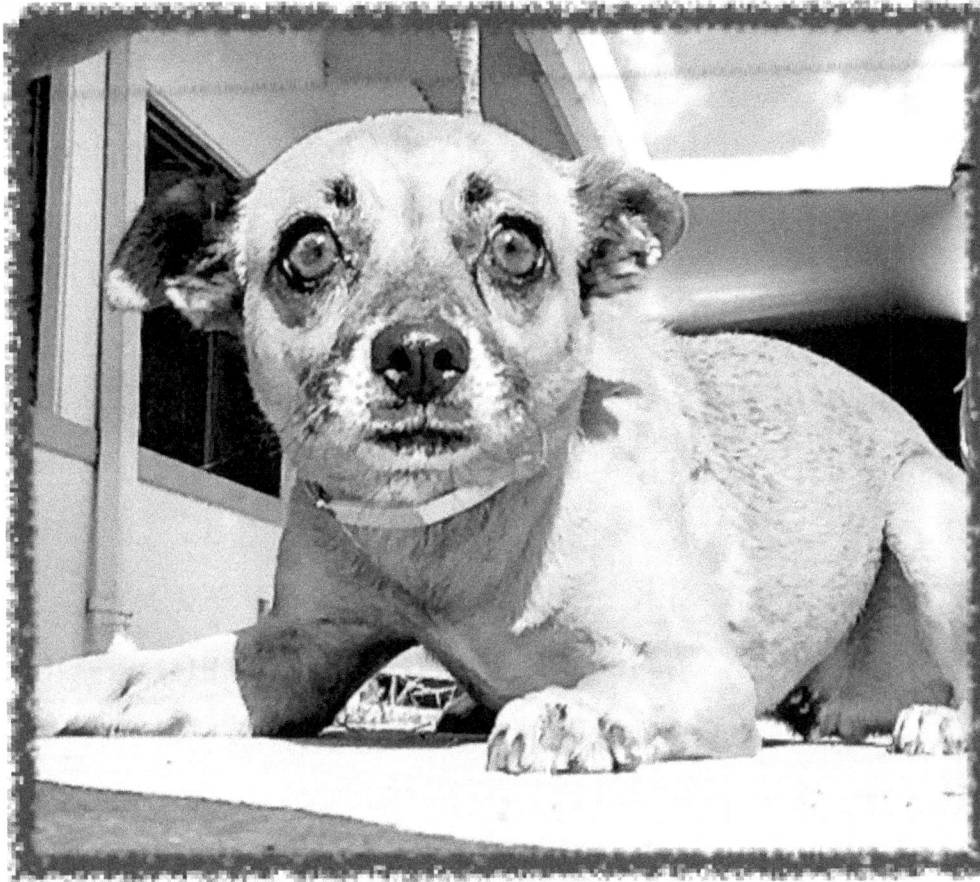

Urgent Status Christmas Dogs Video!

These are the 7 dogs that, needed fosters to save them for Christmas Eve 2014. I don't think that any dog or cat should be put to sleep, on any day, especially not on a holiday! We should work towards not providing this service on special holidays and inform the news media channels about the pets in shelters for more exposure, so that they can find a foster or adopter.

The photos here above, previous and next page are of some of the dogs on the Urgent Status List of Christmas, 2014. We saved all but one of them, the black and white dog on this page. You can see how sick and sad he was in the video. Still breaks my heart to watch him like that. This poor sweet boy had bad discharge and no one came for him. I got into trouble with the director for getting a news station down to the shelter to give them exposure. We are grateful of the support from our local news stations and our Facebook friends. Some of whom came forward to fostered. They are the real heroes here. I also fostered one of them.

Please learn how to help an animal in need in your community by reaching out to your local shelter.

Open your heart to fostering today!

Foster Dog Stories
Cupid

Cupid's Story Video!

Cupid was my first foster dog from Palm Beach County Animal Control. She was one of the Christmas Urgent Status Dogs you just read about. The month before fostering her one of my dogs (Binky) had passed away. This triggered me to take a foster challenge. I was familiar with Cupid from volunteering at the shelter during playgroup sessions. I always noticed she had an excellent temperament with people and other dogs.

Check out what our time together was like in the video above! The music and video was done by me and collaborators. Cupid got adopted and now lives with a woman in Stuart, Florida.

After fostering her, I got involved and tried to save as many dogs as I could, especially the dogs that were on the urgent status list at my local community shelter. I just had to keep them separate from my dogs; change my cloths, disinfect, pick up my hair and wash my hands a lot. Some dogs may be sicker than others. Some dogs may not even notice any symptoms at all.

Maggie

I had a family contact me from a Facebook adoption post on my foster Maggi. They came to meet her the evening before she was due back at Palm Beach County Animal Control shelter. The family had 3 other dogs (one was an amazing 140-pound pitbull) and children. We made a special arrangement for a meet and greet with everybody at the shelter. They adopted Maggi and every once in awhile, I hear from them.

Maggie Meet and Greet at Shelter with Children and Other Dogs Video!

Black Jack

Black Jack's Adoption Video!

I pulled Black Jack from Palm Beach County Animal Care and Control for GTS Husky Rescue. We discovered he had an abnormal finger growth on his hind leg. It was later surgically removed because, it could have gotten caught on something and hurt him. Check out Black Jack's special video. I hope you enjoy!

Foster Toddler

It's good to introduce children properly to dogs by fostering and of course supervision. This is also a good way to try out if you like a dog for keeps while, saving a life at the same time.

Avery

Avery was not showing well at GTS Husky Rescue after arriving from Miami Dade County Animal Services (she was there for 2 months). She was about one year old, small and seriously traumatized. She had shut down emotionally, was very scared and would hide towards the wall away from people and could not interact with people or other dogs. She was afraid of her own shadow. I fostered and worked with her for two and a half months; she was around other normal balanced dogs and going for walks with a training collar and fresh encouraging treats to help keep her from running back home. She walked with her tail tucked in tight. To gain her trust, I encouraged her a lot, got her outside for fresh air and worked with her every chance I could with my helper dogs.

Thanks to social media and Facebook, someone saw one of my posts of Avery. A woman was talking to her neighbor about this little black dog she kept seeing on Facebook. The next thing you know, they filled out an online application. Once the review of the application was complete, we arranged for them to come down to meet Avery. The next trip was us going to visit with them. On March 13, 2015 she was officially adopted! Avery is featured in my other book "**Getting Started on the Right Paw Dog Basic Training**" book under "Placement Training". When we went to visit her new family, we immediately showed her where her "Place" or "Spot" was. They also welcomed her with a custom treat jar with her name on it!

Avery's Beach Adoption Video!

Hannah

Hannah's Beach Adoption Video!

GTS Husky Rescue received "Hannah" from Miami Dade County Animal Services where the animal intake and euthanasia numbers are extremely high! So many dogs come in there, that they often don't know where to put them. Sometimes they would just have to tie or latch them up to a fence waiting to be processed for intake. Hannah was one and a half years old, Golden Retriever. She had just given birth to puppies that were all put to sleep. She was devastated and so scared that, we could not get her to move at all. She would pancake down to the ground in fear. With the help of Avery, who understood what she was going through, and my other helper dogs, over time she started coming out of her shell. She was adopted! Check out her adoption video above filmed in Palm Beach, Florida.

Mamma Oreo and Her 9 Puppies

I was at Animal Control to pick up another dog to foster and asked someone there about the momma dog and her puppies that, they had sent an urgent plea email on a couple of days ago. They said she was still there and if I would like to meet her. When we met we had an immediately connection. I did second guess myself, thinking a momma dog and her 9 puppies, plus my dogs, might have been too much to foster, but what

an awesome experience it was! I always left my house, with a big smile on my face every morning.

Her puppies were brought in first, by Oreo's, owner's father, just a couple days old because, their mom had strayed away from home. Momma Oreo was found tied to a pole in Pahokee, Florida and brought into Palm Beach County Animal Care and Control a couple of days later. The owner called in a few weeks after a while, I was fostering her. She refused to get her sterilized or pay for the violation fees owed to get her back unsterilized. She said that she was out of town taking care of a sick relative and left Oreo with her brother to take care of her.

Momma Oreo and her 9 one week old puppies all caught kennel cough while at the shelter and time was of the essence to get them out!, I fostered and treated them. They had their room separate from my pets. They got plenty of love and attention!

I was able to find them all homes on Facebook and we are all still in touch. Occasionally we have reunions. I love seeing how they have grown up!

Fostering Adoption Promotion Video!
Momma Oreo & her 9 Puppies Playing!
Puppy Grown Up Snorring!
Puppies Distroying Pillows Video!
Puppy's Playing in Bed Video!

Four years later puppy reunion.

Luna

Balck Dogs Happy Birthday Adoption Video!
Black Dog in a Pool of Play Balls!
Black Dog Puppy Reunion Video!
Out of the 9 puppies that belonged to momma Oreo,
only one puppy was returned after 2 months of being

adopted. Luna's first family's toddler was being too aggressive with her. With many tears, she was dropped off back to me. I spent the next 3 months trying to find her the perfect safe home through social media again. Luna's (means moon in Spanish) name was given to her by the family that first adopted her, so they kept it. She is super smart, lots of energy, a very quick learner and very motivated by toys. She loves playing catch and retrieves. She would bring the toy back, sit and look at you intensely to get you to throw it again. Sometimes she did a backward flip if the ball went over her. She learned to crawl on command too! I spent a lot of time just having fun with her. We trained and walked daily. Luna responded well to coconut oil in her diet for her dry skin issues that, she came back with. She must have been just around 6 months old.

Her new family adores her. The picture above is his current forever family! They take her to the park, she goes swimming in the family pool and even goes on boat rides. She came to visit me and her brother occasionally. It was like old times. Luna uses to wear a collar with bells, so I would know where she was at all times. You can see her in one of the videos playing with her brother. We found her a perfect family. Congratulations Luna!

These are the same puppies 5 years later!

Trooper

Pictures where taken on Christmas day! He was adopted the month after. Happy adoption dance for Trooper!

Snow

Snow was fostered and adopted!

Snow's Adoption Video!

Ally

ID #A1737674 She was just returned
from foster. 1 year old. Adopted!
Ally's Adoption Video!

Coco

She was fostered and adopted.
Coco's Adoption Video!

COCO

ttps://www.youtube.com/watch?v=r4DvDYjCgIU

ADOPTED!

Yogi
5 y. Lab,
Palm Beach County
Animal Control

www.everythingdogs.net

Hank

Hank was found with apparent burn wounds on his back, due to acid being poured on his back. He was brought in as a stray to our local community shelter. Blessed Paws Rescue took care of him and found him a awesome home!

Hank's Adoption Video!

Christmas with Chocolate's at the Shelter Video!

Jazzy

Jazzy was 1 year old here. She loves to run around, play catch, play love-bug on your lap and give you her affection! She is only 38 lbs., very small dog.

Jazzy ended up at the Lake County Sheriff Department Shelter with two other English bulldogs. She was spayed there and adopted. She was then returned three days later. She was later transferred to Lady Lake Animal Shelter north of Orlando, Florida. This is an older retirement community and the shelter is small. It is run by volunteers and they had nobody that, was interested in her. A few days later, Blessed Paws Rescue Charity in Lake Worth, Florida received an email about Jazzy and agreed to take her in. The shelter told her that she was

perfectly healthy, but she had a funny way of running; her back feet kicked out to the side a little bit and it almost looked like she was going to fall. It's something that, she was born with, but it didn't bother her. Doctors didn't think it would ever get worse.

Her foster drove to meet a shelter staff member half way. Everyone loved Jazzy's adoption video! You can check her out here with some of my music. Enjoy!

Jazzys Adorable Adoption Video!

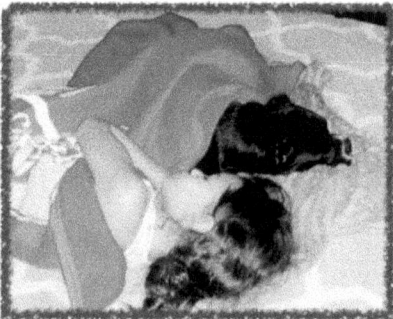

Fenway

Meet gorgeous Fenway! He was 6 years old here, 80 pounds neutered. Great with other dogs, cats, children, crate trained and housebroken. He is an excellent dog! His super awesome foster dad, Steven, had Fenway for 3 months before 2 application verifications did not work out. Fenway now lives in a house full of cats and is loving his new happy forever home!

Fenway's Adoption Video!

Tuffy's Story

Tuffy was thankfully fostered out, due to kennel cough. The day he went into foster he was let out into the back yard and escaped through the hedges. He went missing for 2 weeks. Volunteers put signs up everywhere and looked for him relentlessly. We received a tip that a dog looking like him was seen hanging out by a boat storage lot with a green leash on. This was definitely Tuffy! We set a trap for him, close by with lots of food and kept checking on it for any signs of him. Within 24 hours he was caught. Through The Darbster's Foundation, he was then moved to North Shore Rescue in New England where the sterilization laws are stricter and people don't abandon their pets at such a large rate. North Shore Rescue brings a big bus down to Palm Beach County, Florida and takes the dogs from Peggy Adams Rescue League and The Darbster's Foundation to try to alleviate the over-crowding of the high risk to animals in Palm Beach County. They have taken as many as 30 dogs in one day. These are pictures from a volunteer.

Rodger Dodger

Rodger was found on a vacant field, heartworm positive. He was the first dog to get sponsored for this treatment through the Darbster's Foundation (they raise money through their vegan waterfront bistro. After a very long 6 months at the shelter, Rodger was spinning in his kennel. His mental health was deteriorating and breaking down. He bit the kennel rods till he lost his 3 bottom front teeth. He was very good with other dogs as kennel-mates. However, Rodger did not have socialization skills with people. He did not know how to take treats and bit people's hands by mistake. I was taught how to give treats to him in a special way. By simply going under with treats with your palm open, so that he could see it. This taught him how

to be gentle. He was rehabilitated. He sits and gives you his paw in exchange for treats.

Rodger became famous on Facebook. One year, he opened up for Vanilla Ice at a Christmas event. He was adopted and returned 3 times. I ended up keeping him till he was suffering with Lung cancer I later found out by having a x-ray done on him for a check up that he had 2 pellet inside him from being shot. This could have also explained his behavior sometime. RIP Rodger, Mommy & your siblings love you. Check out his very special rehabilitation adoption video here:

Rodger Dodger's Special Adoption Video!

Puppies Oreo, Mindy, and Coco

When I Got the Girls at the Shelter Video!

I originally went down to animal control because of an email of an urgent status dogs I received. I was on a mission to rescue Oreo (pictured on the left) on her last moment before being put to sleep (because she had Kennel-Cough / CIRD). I then found out she came in with 2 of her sister's, so I ended up taking all three. Their owner had mental issues and his mother could not keep the dogs. I soon found Oreo a home. After she was cleared from the shelter's veterinarian, it took me another month and a half to be able to find both of her sisters homes together in Miami. An adoption application and verification were done, then they came to meet them. I took them down there for a home inspection and they were both adopted for about 6 months. Then Coco Puff and Mindy ate a sofa down to the frame and were returned to me with many tears.

One of them (Mindy) had a very good adoption opportunity in Orlando, Florida, but my husband said if we can't get them both adopted together; that we should keep them. They are living happily with me and my pack of dogs and loving life together!

Coco and Mindy's Adoption Video Collection

Coco & Mindy's Halloween Adoption Video!

Learning to Sit and Stay for Treats Video!

Girl's Adoption Video!

Coco Puff Gets Tummy Rumbs Video!

Obstacle Course - Coco's Adoption Video!

Learning to Pray Before Eating Video!

Girls Sun Bathing With Other Dogs!

Reporting Post Hurrican Mathew Adoption Video!

Girls Sleeping and Playing with Teddybear Video!

Chapter 8
Volunteering

There are many ways to help out animals in your community; by simply volunteering a few hours a week. You will make a world of a difference to the animals that, you come in contact with. Even if you just spend 12 minutes with them, it helps the facility staff members. Unfortunately, the county's designated annual budget for animal services is very limited to help animals.

Volunteering is an excellent way to help animals and meet people that have the same interest as you. You can team up with them to excel in helping animals together. The best reward of all is; these animals will make you smile, nourish your spirit and heart when,

you see how important you are to them. You will be hooked and come back for more. Ask about volunteer programs at your local shelter animal care control services, or search online for a reputable rescue charity organization near you.

CBS "Pet of the Day" with Red Video!

Common Volunteer Positions

- Lost and Found (assisting pet owners with lost and found pets).

- Community Projects and Special Events (volunteer to set up/break down, work displays and events).

- PawpurrazziVolunteer (photographer). You can take profile pictures for social media and possibly put together videos and flyers of pets to assist them in the adoption process.

- Customer Service Greeters (welcomes the public and assists with adoptions).

- Cat Socializing (exercising and socializing cats in the adoption program).

- Volunteering your home and your time to Foster Care.

- Pet Exercise and Play Group Program (walking and socializing the dogs).

- Grooming and bathing dogs.

- Spay Shuttle Client Registration (at the registration table in the mornings).

- Educational Programs and Tours (presenting educational programs at the elementary, middle, and high schools).

- Kennel Care Assistant (caring for and feeding the animals).

- Helping to coordinate adoption/fundraiser events, transportation, grooming, helping out with office work and laundry services.

- Student Volunteer Programs for School Credit

- Adult Court Appointed Community Service

First you would have to sign up and take an *orientation* to see where you may be interested in volunteering. They usually are held in a group once a month. They may need a minimum amount of people to sign up; to hold an orientation with other new volunteers. Please call or go online to find out more. Maybe all you need to do is have a personal interview arranged with the volunteer coordinator.

In some shelters in South Florida, where I'm from, you may encounter seeing other animals like chickens, pigs, rabbits, goats, lamb, cows or horses.

After orientation, you may have to get some additional training or assistance in the field you want to volunteer in, so that you are confident, comfortable, and that everyone is safe.

You will get basic training on shelter's protocols like; how to walk in the kennels, getting dogs out safely and how to handle dogs in different situations. Dogs that have high energy, confined to a small kennel space for long periods of time, can causes them to run away on you at first chance or jump on you. They will prepare you with some basics training so that you know how to handle most situations that you could encounter.

Listing dogs personality detailed information when you are working on the adoption floors on the "Daily Kennel Log Book" can help in getting to know more

about the adoptable dogs, for a better chance of them getting paired up with the right family successfully, or pairing them up with other adoptable dogs as a kennel roommate at the shelter.

Shelters may have restrictions for an adoptable dog demonstrated by a color-coded flag in front of the kennel that, is readily accessible for volunteers to see and read to determine if a dog is a good fit for them to take out that day. A dog or cat may have had surgery and should not get dirty or run around.

Some dogs are dog selective, or may not do well walking past other dogs in the kennel. You should know this before taking a dog out, so the dog

doesn't knock you down or get away from you. It is for everyone's safety. Other dogs may not do well with toys, towels, and blankets because they, can sometimes destroy them and eat them out of boredom, or lack of never being properly introduced to toys. A dog can eat anything that they are not supposed to that, can cause them an obstruction, internal issues, bleeding, blocking or choking should be kept away. This easily can and should be avoided. Some dogs have or develop aggression toward items like toys or food bowls. This is called *resource guarding* and can be dangerous if not handled properly and cautiously, with the right corrections from the beginning, or professional trainer.

If a dog is in a shelter's kennel for a long time, they may start to shut down by developing many behavior issues like: mental health deteriorated as a result of many elements of their over-stressed environment days in and out! Dogs are scared. They don't get the exercise, love or training they need to be balanced dogs. Some dogs may jump, or spin in circles, compulsively jump or bite the kennel rods (this causes dogs to loosen or damage their teeth like one of my foster Rodger). Dogs may experience detachment by facing a wall, or develop pancake behavior syndrome where the dog won't get up and move; they just shut down. Many dogs are also dealing with separation anxiety issues where they miss their owners and think they are coming back for them. They are constantly looking for them when you take them out. Many of them come in with prior health issues. Heartworms (cost about $700 or more to treat, depend on where you go), and kennel cough is very common. These dogs get very depressed while at the shelter. Dogs develop skin and hair coat issues from stress and/or cleaning chemicals. In addition to not having a soft padded bed or a spot to rest to offers protection for them getting contaminated with strong cleaning chemicals and hard floors; it causes dogs to develops inflamed raw skin and sores pads too.

I strongly encourage volunteers with experience handling dogs to get involved in Playgroups aka: Playing for Life Animal Enrichment Program. This is when many dogs are introduced to other dogs in small groups to get some exercise and taught how to socialize with each other. You can team up with other volunteers to get all the dogs out from the adoption floor in small groups and in about 2 to 3 hours. Some dogs may take longer to introduce to other dogs and may get time out, while they watch how the other dogs interact with one another. This is an awesome program because dogs get to run around to let all the stress out from being cooped up in a kennel and can offer some ease to relax their mind and body. I will soon show and tell you more about playgroups later in this book!

At my local shelter Palm Beach County Animal Care and Control, the Kennel 1 building is the main dog adoption floor. With 50 kennels, most of them have 2 dogs in each kennel. So that is easily around 80 dogs total, give or take on the day. The enrichment skills that, are taught to volunteers, help socialize the dogs to do better, during their potential adoption meet and greet session. For example: how to sit or take treats. This has increases successful adoption rates, by reducing adoption return numbers in shelters. This also allows us to pair dogs successfully to be good kennel roommates with other dogs safely. Shelters can maximize space by occupying 2 dogs in one kennel if they can get along. With smaller dogs or puppies, sometimes kennels may have even more pooches in them, giving that the dogs get along well together. This is

more common with smaller dogs or puppies. Saving space in a kill shelter saves lives.

Next to Kennel 1, is the Kennel 2 building with another 50 to 80 dogs. Most of which are in their 10-day hold for their owners to come find them and take them home but that, is not the case for most of these dogs. Then there is Kennel 3 that, is for dogs that are in quarantine in another area with other types of animals. It's also used for animals that have just come in as a stray/found, or that have just been surrendered by their owners and need medical and dog training assessment.

In Kennel 2, we have dogs that ended up at the shelter for one reason or another that, are waiting for their 10 day hold to be up. If no one comes forward to claim them, then they are moved to the main adoption floor in Kennel 1 to try to get them adopted before they come down with: kennel cough, develop behavioral issue or time runs out. Which unfortunately the case for many of them.

As more dogs are coming in, some are in isolation or waiting to be evaluated. All these dogs ultimately

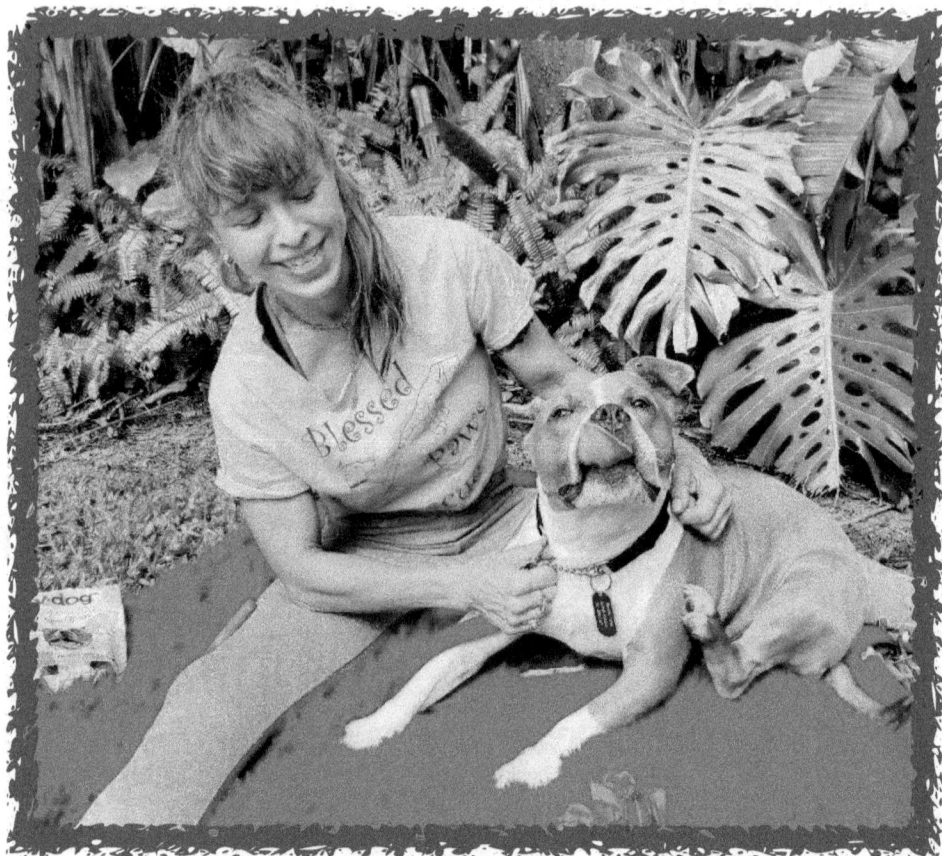

need to get to the Kennel 1 adoption floor with the other dogs that, are ready to get adopted.

If the dog that, is adopted is already sterilized, they can go to their new home the same day, or they are immidiately schedule for surgery and then they can go to their furever safe home.

All dogs get sterilized in Palm Beach County and legal dog guardians are responsible for to pay the fee for breeding or for not spaying or neutering their dogs or cats.

Shelter explicitly expresses to all the volunteers and the public that, their obligation of fairness is to treat all animals equally in regard to available space and time. This system is placed in consideration new animals coming into the communitie's shelter system that, are deserving of the same and equal opportunity to provide shelter food and help them find a loving home for adoption.

Basic Shelter Needed Donations List

Donations are always needed for animals in your community. You or your business can donate money online, phone or by donating basic necessities. You can always get a list from local shelters or rescues near you. Here are some of the basics that they could use:

- Water and food bowls
- Wet dog/cat food
- Dry dog/cat food
- Clumping cat litter
- Non-clay cat litter (for kittens and post-op cats).
- Dog/cat treats

- Toys
- Leashes and collars
- Brushes/grooming tool
- Pet beds
- Cleaning supplies (call your shelter and ask what cleaning supplies it uses/needs).
- Old newspapers
- Paper towel and toilet paper rolls
- Old towels and blankets
- Hand sanitizer
- Office supplies
- Donate a place in your home - by fostering!

I hope this information will get you started on the right paw. This chapter will show you some of the many creative ways we are making a difference by helping out our furry friends in our community.

Volunteer Extravaganza Day!

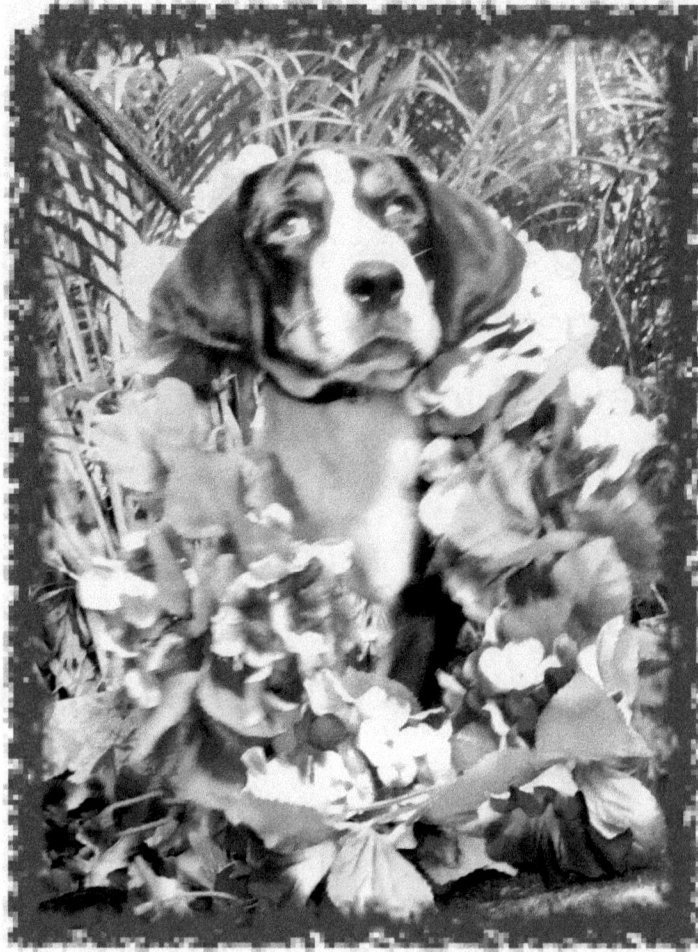

Palm Beach County Animal Care and Control honors and awards shelter volunteers. While offering adoptable dogs an opportunity to: get out of their kennels, learn for a few tricks, have some fun and to possibly get adopted. On this, we got all of our adoptable dogs out to play and do obstacle courses for prizes and treats. We gave awards to dogs for best behaved, best dressed and agility course skills.

This was an excellent event! Check out this video link to see what it was like!

Volunteer Extravaganza Day Video!

Here are some Memorial Day videos of washing and prepping dogs for sterilization, get them ready for "Count Down to Zero Mega Adoption Event" at the West Palm Beach Convention Center. Please watch!

Amber's Outreach Rescue Puppy Bowl Video

Happy Labor Day Sun Glasses Video!

Volunteer Washing Dogs Report Video!

Paws in the Park Adoption Event Video!

Memorial Dog Wash Video!

The previous page is Blue saying, "Happy Memorial Day!" He was returned to the shelter with his brother after being adopted 5 months prior. He was adopted again!

Easter Day Parade Video!

Paws on the Park, West Plam Beach Dog Activity Video!

Momma Lily still trying to find a home Video!

Sam Spot the Tripod Dog

Here I'm featuring Sam Spot the tripod cattle dog on his adoption adventure to CBS Channel 12 station and film "Pet of the Day." He belonged to a farmer as a working, herding, cattle dog. One day while, doing his rounds, he had an accident that caused him to lose his left front leg. He was six years old here excellent with other dogs and children. He gets around just with some effort and is a smart love-bug. Sam Spot is now adopted; thanks to Kibblez of Love Pet Food Bank and Rescue! Check out our time together and how he got around.

Sam's Adoption Adventure Video!

Playgroup

Playgroup Fall 2018 Video!

A Great Playgroup Day!

Playgroup, also known as "Dogs Playing for Life", was founded by Aimee Sadler. She has introduced a

playgroup system and currently has 25 years of experience working within the entertainment industry and animal shelters. She has many professional accomplishments and attends national and regional welfare conferences. She put this program together for the welfare of animals in a shelter environment with the hopes of preventing animals from emotionally shutting down or showing signs of aggression, once placed in a shelter. Her methods have proven a 95% release rate in the canine achievement for adoptions within the administration shelters.

A dog's natural instinct is to play, travel, walk and be in movement. Playgroup is a critical enrichment and assessment tool for shelters! This is so important when it comes to introducing or socializing with other dogs. Many times dogs will need to be paired up in a

kennel with another dog to save room in the shelter and to save a life. In other words, this helps animals get along and do well in the shelter environment, instead of breaking down. When a dog breaks down; you will see scratching, eating the walls, jumping severely, detachment, facing the wall away from people and shutting down.

Aimee travels around to training shelters promoting safety protocols for both people and the animals. She emphasizes and ensures that playgroups will bring out the best in a shelter dog. It will reduce the risk of fighting and protect them from possible

injuries. Her staff provides visits and implements "Playgroup" to the new volunteers when training dogs on the adoption floor. She wants to get all the dogs out from the adoption kennel and is very passionate about the program. Volunteers are also provided training on evaluating each dog in learning their true personality. Exercise and social-behavioral skills are put in place to assist a dogs' successful adoption for a furever home.

The ASPCA and the Petco Foundation have joined forces with "Dogs Playing for Life" to improve the quality of life for shelter dogs with structured playgroups.

By collaborating and getting awarded a generous grant of $1.5 million to "Dogs Playing for Life" is used for interactive play groups to help socialize, evaluate and change the lives of shelter dogs. They hope it can help introduce this new innovative playgroup enrichment training to shelters country-wide.

I encourage everyone to familiarize themselves with their local animal shelters and sign up to volunteer, foster, donate or adopt. Take some basic training classes with them and learn how to get dogs out of kennel per the shelter's protocol.

When you get involved with training and/or volunteering; keep notes of the dogs that you work with. This helps us to keep them safe and to learn more about them. Working with experienced trainers will make you more confident, till you are ready to work with dogs on your own. Usually, we have a few runners pulling out dogs from the kennels safely while others may be in the yard working with the dogs, or perhaps logging information updates notes about the animals. This should be done with a minimum of 3 people in a small group. Dogs that do not do well are marked and color-coded with labels, for instance; a purple label means: surgery, a green label means: the dog does not do well with toys or blankets and a blue label means: the dog does not like other dogs. It's important for trainers and volunteers to understand the systems in place, and to practice safety during playgroup sessions at all times.

dogsplayingforlife.com

Sunday Playgroup at Shelter Video

Chapter 9
Pitbulls in the United States

Frankie's Story Adoption Video!

Sella's Story

Stella's Story Video!

Stella With Baby Video!

Stella had a "last call" notice (to be put to sleep) because she came down with kennel cough (CIRD). I fostered her, trained her, got her better and I was able to find her an awesome family. Happy dance! I changed her name from Goodie to Margo because she, seemed to respond better to it, and named her after one of the

shelter's trainers that, was very helpful to me. She was excellent on the leash; no pulling at all. I posted her special adoption video on my local yoga studio's Facebook page, right before her time was up for a check-up with the shelter veterinarian, to get her back on the adoption floor. Very fortunate for her, one of the teachers fell in love with her at first sight when she saw her video! She came over with her family and their newborn baby. Stella immediately responded well with her calm gentle temperament. It was apparent that there was an awesome connection. Pitbulls are known as, nanny/granny dogs that, take care of children and are a reliable member of the family. *Look at this same baby boy (growing up together as best friends) holding hands together while watching a hockey game, on the previous page.*

Pitbull History

In the 16th century, nearly every town in England had baiting ring. The popularity of baiting events was unparalleled at the time, as they could draw spectators from every level of society. Their popularity was further enhanced by the misguided perception that prolonged torture ensured the tenderness of the dog's meat.

By 1853, bull baiting was deemed illegal and the uses of these dogs turned for more practical hunting, herding and protection qualities. Also during this time, two integral events in the history in the use of the American Pit Bull Terrier occurred; the bubonic plague broke out and the practice of "ratting" became popular.

The bubonic plague was also of great concern killing millions worldwide. It was often spread by rats harboring fleas that carried infection. A good ratting dog on the farm was used to control rodent populations and in many cases was paramount for human survival. The sport of ratting soon caught the eye of noblemen and people of economic industry and wealth.

Any blocky headed dog or any mix of breeds that is between 35 and 100 pounds (upwards of 30 individual dog breeds) may currently fall in this broad category.

- The dog "genome" consists of approximately 20,000 genes.

- A variation across 50 genes determines the breed's defining physical traits.

Famous Pitbulls

If you take a look back at our history with Pitbulls, you will see that, we have had a very positive relationship with them. For instance, how we have so many famous Pitbulls like:

Pete - AKA "Petey" was a character played by father and son Pitbulls in the *"Little Rascals"*, during the 1930s. He was known by the "ring around his eye". that was circled in by the Hollywood make-up

artist "Max Factor" by; adding it on and credited as an oddity in *"Ripley's Believe It or Not."*

Nipper - In the 1890s, Nipper served as the model for a painting titled *"His Master's Voice."* This image was the basis for the dog and gramophone logo used by several audio recordings and associated brands like RCA.

Bud - In 1903 was the first dog to take a cross-country drive with his owner.

Sergeant Stubby (1916 - March 16, 1926) - A hero known to captured the hearts of the nation. Over the years, he became known as the beloved symbol of the Americana in World War I. He is the official mascot of the 102nd Infantry Regiment United

States Army, and was assigned to the 26th (Yankee) Division in World War I. He served for 18 months and participated in seventeen battles on the Western Front. He saved his regiment from surprise mustard gas attacks, found and comforted the wounded and once caught a German soldier by the seat of his pants; holding him there until American soldiers found him. His actions were well-documented in contemporary American newspapers.

Spuds MacKenzie - Is a fictional dog character created for use in extensive advertising campaign marketing Bud Light beer in the late 1980's.

Bullseye (formerly known as Spot) - Is a Bull Terrier and the official mascot of the Target Corporation.

Breed Specific Legislation (BSL)

This is a law passed by a legislative body on specific breed or breeds of domesticated animals. Some jurisdictions have enacted breed-specific legislation in response to a number of well-publicized incidents involving in the 80's, of other dog breeds commonly used in dogfighting. This legislation ranges from outright bans on the possession of these dogs, to restrictions and conditions on ownership. This often establishes a legal presumption that these dogs are prima facie legally "dangerous or vicious."

In response, some state-level governments in the United States have prohibited or restricted the ability of municipal governments within those states to enact breed-specific legislation.

• In 1980, Hollywood, Florida's City Commission passed an ordinance that required people who owned Pitbull dogs to complete special registration forms and prove the possession of $25,000 public liability insurance.

• The regulation applied to several breeds collectively identified as Pitbulls. In 1984, a New

Mexico town completely banned Pitbulls, and allowed county officers to confiscate and euthanize the dogs.

- Also that year, Cincinnati, Ohio enacted a regulation that "defined vicious dogs" to include all Pitbull terriers, and put special restrictions on the confinement, sale, and control of these dogs which did not apply to other breeds.

- In each of these situations, one breed of dog has been singled out as "inherently dangerous to society", regardless of the individual dog's present or past behavior. Reference: animallaw.info

- **700 cities ban Pitbulls.** Many families have been affected by this. When the law is changed, family pets are taken from them and are put to sleep. This is because irresponsible dog owners and dog fighters are exposed by the media; making them a media hot button. They should be focusing on all positives that, outweigh the all of incidences that this specific breed has had. They get judged in a very general description by their genetic appearance.

• In fact "small breed dogs" bite more often than Pitbulls do! Something else the media doesn't mention is that "Pitbulls" increases viewers. The media veers from equally covering all the facts and does not usually tell us the full story when it's aired.

• When an animal attacks, they may have legitimate reasons to react to a strangers that way like: they were scared. They always give you a warning. We need to recognize it. Screaming, strange noise and kids harassing dogs can be very provoking to any dog that, can sets them off to attack!

- Many dog owners don't: socialize, or make early corrections with their dogs' behaviors, or secure their property; so they can't get out. When you own any breed of dog, you are responsible to make sure they are safe and that you work towards having a socialized well-balanced dog.

Chips Special Adoption Video!

Dog Fighting
Shelter Dogs Video!

Animal fighting has been brought to the forefront of the nation's attention by the highly publicized conviction of NFL star quarterback Michael Vick's 2001 - 2007 "The Dogfighting Operation."

On April 25, 2007, the state investigations found the men tested the dogs in fights, then shot, electrocuted or hung dogs; who did not perform well.

On, or about April 2007, *Peace, Phillips, and Vick* executed approximately 8 dogs that did not perform well in 'testing' sessions by various methods; including; hanging, drowning and slamming at least one dog's body to the ground.

A report by a U.S. Department of Agriculture (USDA) investigator provided more details on the April 2007 killings, saying that, "the men hung approximately three dogs by placing a nylon cord over a 2 X 4 that was nailed to two trees located next to the big shed. They also drowned approximately three dogs by putting the dogs' heads in a five-bucket of water. They killed one dog by slamming it to the ground several times before it died, breaking the dog's back or neck." According to a witness, the men fought their trained Pitbulls with pet dogs and they "thought it was funny to watch the Pitbull dogs belonging to Bad Newz Kennels injure or kill the other dogs."

May 22, 2007, Defenders of Dogfighting
In a news interview reported by the Associated Press that two other football players defended Vick and ridiculed the idea that dogfighting is a crime.

The Eagles signed Vick in 2009, very soon after he served a 21-month federal prison sentence for dogfighting conspiracy and was then reinstated by the NFL. The Pittsburgh Steelers, on Aug 2015, signed a 1-year deal for 13 seasons in the league. The New York Jets signed Michael Vick to a $5 million contract in 2015. In August 2011, Vick signed a 6 year $100 million contracts with the Philadelphia Eagles. This new contract includes $40 million in guaranteed cash that works out to an annual salary of $16.5 million.

Vick is now the third athlete, joining Derek Jeter and Shaquille O'Neal, in the history of professional sports to sign more than $100 million-plus in contracts. Vick's original $130 million contracts with the Atlanta Falcons was negated after his legal troubles. In 2012, Michael Vick was estimated to be worth $16 million.

Snow's Adoption Video!

**Sisters
Coco Puff
& Mindy**

Petey

Petey is a low rider about 48 pounds, 2 1/2 year old, male completely potty trained. He is a love bug with other dogs, especially little dogs, cats and people. Rides great in a car, low energy.

Petey's Adoption Video!

Animal Welfare Act and Regulations

The Animal Welfare Act (AWA) requires that minimum standards of care and treatment be provided for certain animals bred for commercial sale, used in research, transported commercially, or preventing and punishing animal abuse, cruelty and neglect are largely the responsibilities of the individual states.

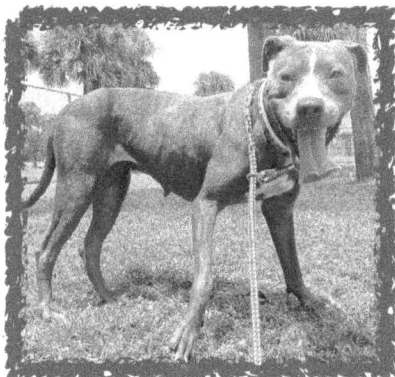  

COWBOY
A1752184

BLUE
A1723916

GATACUS
A1744846

MAJOR
A1616974 12/3/13

RAIN
A1723456

DAMIAN
A1743103

DARLA
A1751891 11/3/14

WHITEY
A1717673 Pit M 2 y

Pitbulls Have Millions of Adorable Faces to Love!

Duke

ID #A192919, 2 year-old, excellent with other dogs, sweet, very smart, loves to play catch and retrieve. He was finally adopted after a long time at the shelter!

Duke's Adoption Video!

Federal Tracking of
Cruelty Cases

In 2014, the FBI announced that it will <u>add cruelty to animals as a category in the agency's Uniform Crime Report</u>, a nationwide crime-reporting system. While only about a third of U.S. communities currently participate in the system, the data generated will help create a clearer picture of animal abuse and guide strategies for intervention and enforcement. Data collection began in January 2016, and will cover four categories: simple/gross neglect, intentional abuse and torture, organized abuse (such as dogfighting and cockfighting) and animal sexual abuse.

Who Abuses Animals

Cruelty and neglect across socio-economic boundaries. The media reports suggest that animal abuse is common in both rural and urban areas. Intentional cruelty to animals is strongly correlated with other crimes, including violence against people. Serious animal neglect (such as seen in cases of animal hoarding) is often an indicator of people in need of social or mental health services. Surveys suggest that those who intentionally abuse animals are predominantly male and under 30 while those involved in animal hoarding are more likely to be female and over 60 (Lockwood, 2008).

Most Common Victims

The animals whose abuse is most often reported are dogs, cats, horses and livestock. Based on numbers from pet-abuse.com, of 1,880 cruelty cases reported in the media in 2007:

- 64.5 percent (1,212) involved dogs, (25 percent of these were identified as Pitbull-type breeds).

- 18 percent (337) involved cats and 25 percent (470) involved other animals.

Ghost's Adoption Video!

KING

Organized Cruelty and Dog Fighting

50 states currently including felony provisions in their animal cruelty laws. Before 1986, only four states had felony animal cruelty laws: Massachusetts (1804), Oklahoma (1887), Rhode Island (1896), and Michigan (1931). Three states enacted felony laws in the 1980s, 19 states in the 1990s and 25 more since 2000 (including the District of Columbia). First vs. second offense in some state laws only allows felony charges if the perpetrator has a previous animal cruelty conviction. Given that only a fraction of animal cruelty acts are ever reported or successfully prosecuted, The HSUS believes all states should allow felony charges for

egregious cruelty, regardless of whether the perpetrator has a prior conviction.

Frankie

Bart

BART

A1921085, 2 years old, super sweet, affectionate, smart & excellent with other dogs.
Palm Beach County Animal Control.
Come meet him fall in Love!

ID # A1921085, brindle, 2 years old, very smart and affectionately good with other dogs. He was pulled by a local rescue.

Bart's Adoption Video at the Shelter!

Honey and Sadie

Both in K-112 Sadie - ID #A1712477, was not in the log-book, and Honey ID #A1711418 pit mix 12/30/13.

Angelina

Rosco and Mocha

Roscoe on the left and Mocha are siblings. They where with Kibbles of Love Pet Food Bank and Rescue for over a year before getting separately adopted. Roscoe was returned.

Mocha's Adoption Video! and **Rosco's Adoption Video**

Marble

Mable from Palm Beach County Animal Control was pulled out by a rescue organization in Orlando. They got him a foster with no experience that, allowed their children to scare him. They called the Orlando Animal Control Services to pick him up. His previous foster drove a few hours out and then back to get him. We were able to find him his forever family!

Honey

ID #A1701323

Chance

Chance's Adoption Video.

Chance was found on a vacate property when I was asked to help him out and started posting him. He was fostered many times and ended up at the shelter. One time he got adopted from the shelter and got returned because the community he moved into had breed restriction. He was good with other dogs and cats. We got a couple more fosters and then adopted again. Two weeks after being adopted, they had trouble with the children hitting him and they called local animal services to pick him up. His 3rd foster was a champ to pick him up and bring him back down from a 3-hour drive each way and was soon adopted through social media. Chance spend that holiday by a Christmas tree with his ew furever home. Chance now has a dog sister!

Peral

ID #A1734462 K1-120 American Staff, loves to run around.

Pearl's Adoption Video!

Vance

ID #A1704717 pitbull terrier, 1 year, 7 months, brindle, neutered. On 10/25/13, he was owner surrendered. On 11/7/13, he was fostered and back on the adoption floor 3/21/14, and then adopted out on 3/21/14.

Nina

ID #A1594997 5 years old, brindle, blue nose. Found on Benoist Farms Road on 8/18/12. RTO (returned over the counter) on 5/23/13. Then adopted on 6/13/13, then on 10/28/13, she was found stray and RTO. I understand that she was adopted again!

Bentley

ID #A1767325 pitbull, male 6 years old, unaltered, 39 lbs., good with other dogs, cats, kids and housebroken.

Foster Failure

Rodger Enoying the Sofa Video!

Fargo

ID# A1721299 pitbull, male, 3 years old, found with a blue-collar on 2/27/14, on Snapper Way in Delray Beach, Florida. He was then fostered on 3/16/14. On 3/29/14, he was brought back in the shelter, and then on 5/25/14, he was put to sleep because of observed behavior issues.

Open your heart to fostering, volunteering, donating to veterinarian research, sterilization or adopting a shelter or rescue dog or cat today!

Zimba

K1-118 ID #A1737916 gray, male, 3 years old. Did not want to go back into his kennel.

Gravey

K1-131 -ID #A1689471 very smart, plays catch well, great listener. He was found on Collier Road in West Palm Beach, FL and was a

Marble
Palm Beach Animal Care and Control alumni.

Shelter Pitbull Faces

KING
A1735517

CHAKI
A1729407

GORY
1760008

JERSEY
A1745304

SENA - 5/26/13
hand walk special
request. 3 years old,
beautiful

NINA
A1594997
7/22/13

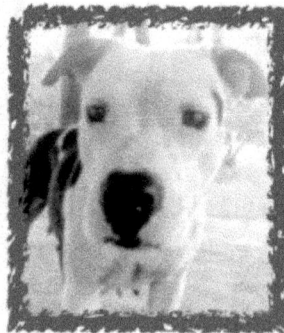

"MOO" - Just had
puppies but not in
kennel with her,
12/01/13.

**Frankie
Rescued**

CARLA-
A1735221, F, 2y,
sweet, obedient.

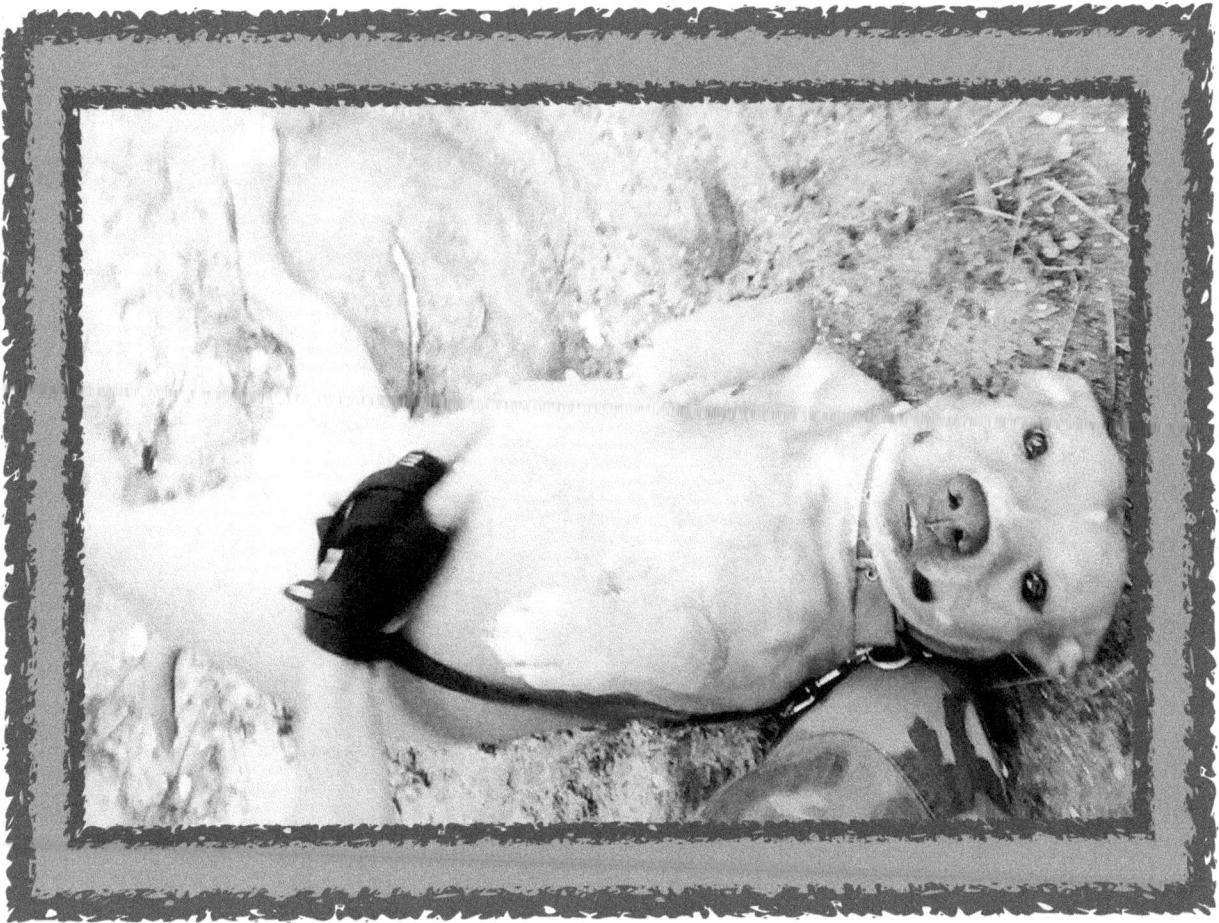

Yari

Yari's
Adoption
Video

Happy Adoption Pictures

AVERY HANK KIMI SNOW VONDA

BLUE REUNION MOOKIE SAMI NENE

RODGER PRIMA HANK COCO CHARLIE & QUEENIE

PRIMA

MAX RHALO MOMMA OREO BUTCH MIA ICE CREAM ADOPTION AT PBCACC LOBBY

PUPPY REUNION PARTY JAZZY ATHENA DUTCHIE MASH POTATO JAZZY FENWAY

DELILAH CHANCE ELSA STELLA CALVIN

3 KITTENS ADOPTION LUIGI & SOPHIE COCO BEAN CAROL CAROL

Good-Bye

Thank you for reading my book. I appreciated you spending time to learn more about dogs. They mean the world to me!

We need to help animals in shelters, rescues and everywhere that we can. Let's live in harmony on our journey into the future, alongside all kinds of creatures on this earth.

I wish everyone, happy dog guardianship, knowledge, safety, health, love, happy memories and harmony on your journey into future living alongside your furry friends and family members!

Open your heart to fostering, volunteering, donating for more veterinarian medical research, sterilizing, advocating and adopting a shelter dog!

Check out my other dog education books part of the Everything Dogs Book Collection

By Mercy Lopez

www.everythingdogs.net

SAVING SHELTER
DOGS

TRUE SHELTER DOG STORIES FOSTERING, VOLUNTEERING,
& EVERYTHING YOU WANT TO KNOW TO RESCUE DOGS

The Truth About Animal Shelters Dogs Documented in Picture and Video Stories Links, Intakes, Euthanasia, Statistics, Fostering, Volunteering, Lost, Stray and Found Dog, Anti-Tethering Law, What We are Doing to Bring Our Animal Intake and Euthanasia Numbers Down, Sterilization, High-Risk Animals, Back Dog Syndrome, Kennel-Mates, Pitbull History, Breed Specific Legislation, How we are saving lives in our communities, and more!

Everything Dogs Book Series Collection
•Saving Shelter Dogs
•Getting Started on the Right Paw Basic Dog Training
• Dog Holistic Health Maintenance and Remedies Encyclopedia

By Mercy Lopez

www.everythingdogs.net

www.ingramcontent.com/pod-product-compliance
Lightning Source LLC
LaVergne TN
LVHW061248060426
835508LV00018B/1540